FLAVOURS OF THE SUN

Also by Patricia Lousada

THE DINNER PARTY BOOK

FLAVOURS OF
THE SUN

Patricia Lousada and Charlotte Fraser

MICHAEL JOSEPH
LONDON

MICHAEL JOSEPH

Published by the Penguin Group
27 Wrights Lane, London W8 5TZ
Viking Penguin Inc., 375 Hudson Street, New York, New York 10014, USA
Penguin Books Australia Ltd, Ringwood, Victoria, Australia
Penguin Books Canada Ltd, 10 Alcorn Avenue, Toronto, Ontario, Canada M4V 3B2
Penguin Books (NZ) Ltd, 182–190 Wairau Road, Auckland 10, New Zealand

Penguin Books Ltd, Registered Offices: Harmondsworth, Middlesex, England

First published in Great Britain 1994

Copyright © Patricia Lousada and Charlotte Fraser 1994

All rights reserved.
Without limiting the rights under copyright
reserved above, no part of this publication may be
reproduced, stored in or introduced into a retrieval system,
or transmitted, in any form or by any means (electronic, mechanical,
photocopying, recording or otherwise) without the prior
written permission of both the copyright owner and
the above publisher of this book

Typeset by Datix International Limited, Bungay, Suffolk
Set in 11½/13 pt Monophoto Apollo
Printed in England by Clays Ltd, St Ives plc

ISBN 0 7181 3744 2

The moral right of the authors has been asserted

CONTENTS

Line drawings by Nadine Wickenden

Dishes That Can Be Prepared in Advance

Dishes That Can Partly Be Prepared in Advance

INTRODUCTION

This book has been inspired, and coloured, by the foods of the Mediterranean. The aromatic flavours of fresh vegetables, herbs and fish and their accompanying accents of fragrant olive oils, garlic and anchovies have provided a vivid palette of tastes and textures from which to work. Though drawn from no specific country, the recipes owe much to the sun-filled cuisines of Southern Italy and Sicily, Provence and Valencia. This book has also been influenced by the new thinking about food and health being practised by enlightened cooks and chefs everywhere. Heavy meals structured around meats and creamy sauces have given way to lighter, more spontaneous combinations of vegetables with fish or fowl and grains, with much of it enhanced by delicious and cholesterol-free extra virgin olive oil.

Despite the fact that we are many miles from olive groves and herb-covered hills, a feeling of the south can be captured with the produce now available in Britain. Fresh herbs, fine oil and garlic can lift even northern-grown aubergines and peppers. And those little tinned anchovies packed in olive oil go just as well with farmed salmon or fish from the Atlantic. The trick is to keep an eye out and buy the freshest produce you can, using as many seasonal ones as possible. Armed with good ingredients, the best way to use them is often the simplest, which also means less work for the cook. As you will see, grilling or baking works wonders with vegetables. In the summer when there is an abundance of choice and it is possible to find sun-ripened tomatoes and other well-flavoured vegetables, the joys of this style of cooking can really be appreciated and explored.

Flavours of the Sun contains a good number of fish, poultry and game recipes, but we have kept away from red meat. With so many other options it is much easier now to do without it. Some egg dishes have been included. They are a wonderful source of protein and a versatile base for onion tarts or savoury frittatas. Our main focus, however, has been on vegetables, with their vibrant tastes and colours. We have used them alone or grouped in delicious combinations: aubergines with pesto, leeks with mushrooms, avocado and papaya, peppers with tuna, squid and sun-dried tomatoes...but always with an emphasis on keeping cooking methods light and flavours fresh and decisive. In looking to Italy we have included pizzas, pastas and risottos, which not only provide satisfying backgrounds for more robust tastes and fruity olive oils, but are also in themselves such inexpensive and healthy foods.

Desserts are where we have indulged ourselves and abandoned both calorie and cholesterol counts. Sun-ripened fruit is an unbeatable choice for dessert, but that needs no cookery book. So we have included some delicious, and rather rich, puddings for the times when a great sweet is wanted.

A last word of advice for getting the best from this cookery book. Do invest in a quality olive oil. In France and Italy oil is as prized a possession as fine wine, and by comparison will enrich great numbers of meals. A beautifully scented olive oil is not only good for the heart but, more importantly, it also adds to the pleasures of the table.

Authors' Note
All of the recipes in this book give ingredients in both Imperial (oz, pt, etc.) and Metric (g, ml, etc.) measures. In any one recipe use either set of quantities but not a mixture of both. All teaspoon and tablespoon measurements are level; 1 teaspoon = 5 ml and 1 tablespoon = 15 ml.

Double asterisks (**) in the recipes indicate the point to which they can be prepared in advance. A complete list of the recipes that can be prepared wholly or partly in advance appears on pages vii–x.

INGREDIENTS

Anchovies

Most of the anchovies we buy here are prepared in olive oil and are ready to use. Those packed in glass jars enable you to see what you are buying, but you can also use a good brand of anchovies in small tins. If you can find them whole and packed under salt they will be meatier, and more delicious, but they need to be well rinsed and then skinned, boned and stored in olive oil before use.

Aubergines

The newer varieties, including the Dutch aubergine which you are likely to find here, need no preliminary salting if they are cooked immediately after being cut. Always buy firm shiny ones with unwithered stalks.

Balsamic Vinegar

Aceto balsamico comes from the Italian province of Modena. It is made from the boiled-down must of white grapes and aged in wooden containers for at least ten years. It is a rich brown colour and has a sweet yet sour taste. There are many grades and ages of this special vinegar and the better qualities have a depth and mellowness of flavour that are a wonderful bonus to many dishes.

Bouquet Garni

A basic bouquet garni is made from a few sprigs of parsley, one of thyme and a bay leaf. Cooks today often wrap up the parcel with a roll of leek and, depending on its use, add aromatics such as tarragon or other fresh herbs or a piece of dried orange peel.

Butter

Butter in this book always means unsalted.

Dried Porcini

Dried porcini (*Boletus edulis*; *cèpes* in France) have such an intense rich mushroom flavour that even a few will make a difference in mushroom dishes. They are often sold in small transparent packets. Choose the larger and paler coloured slices and avoid the dark brown smaller pieces. Keep the packets tightly sealed and refrigerated. To reconstitute: pour boiling water over them and soak for 30 minutes, then rub them under cold running water to remove any grit. Strain the soaking water through a sieve lined with kitchen paper and use as directed. Other types of dried mushrooms such as chanterelles or shiitake are very good but have a completely different taste and should not be substituted for dried porcini.

Garlic

There are many types and sizes of garlic. They range in colour from the more usual white to pink and mauve, and their flavours are as varied as their size. Whatever the type, all garlic will be at its sweetest and juiciest when fresh. As it ages it becomes drier and acquires sharpness. You can use the new season's garlic lavishly but be very sparing with older cloves. When using older garlic, cut the cloves in half, and if there is a green centre sprout, discard it – it will be bitter. If the garlic is sprouting from the top it should not be used.

Harissa

This is a paste made from red chillis, garlic and olive oil. It is imported from North Africa and can be found in specialist food stores. It varies in strength, so it should be used with caution.

Herbs

Fresh herbs are used in most of the recipes in this book. They are widely available from greengrocers and supermarkets, and it is also easy to grow your own. Most herbs will flourish in pots and take up very little space – even a windowsill will do.

Olive Oil

The difference between olive oils is startling. Their colours range from pale golden to a rich green and their distinct flavours and textures have prompted a vocabulary almost as fanciful as that used for wine. Like wine they also vary from year to year depending on the climate. There is no doubt that single estate-produced olive oil or small co-operatives which use the old stone mills and traditional methods of production make the best oil. Very little oil is extracted by the first cold pressing and it is therefore expensive, but is in a class of its own and well worth the cost. French olive oil may have *fabrication artisanale* as well as *première pression à froid* on the label. (A delicious one is Huile d'Olive de la Vallée des Baux.) As these oils are expensive, use them only for salads or pouring over vegetables, pastas, pizzas, etc.

Centrifuge technology, used for most commercial olive oil, has meant that a large quantity of oil can be pressed from the olives in only one pressing. This oil bears the label extra virgin olive oil if the oleic acid is one per cent or less. Most of the olive oil we find here fits into this category and although it is labelled extra virgin it covers an enormous range of quality. Try several small bottles of different extra virgin olive oils before investing in a larger amount. Any olive oil that isn't extra virgin should be avoided. Olive oil is perishable. Use it within a year and keep it tightly closed in a cool dark cupboard.

Peppers

Red and yellow peppers are far more succulent than the green and are better for grilling. It is truly well worth the bother of grilling peppers: it gives them a wonderful flavour, improves their digestibility, and softens them. Place them under a hot grill until they blacken on all sides. Then either put them in a covered bowl or pop them into a plastic or paper bag until they are cool enough so you can peel off the charred skin.

Squid

Buy squid that still have their very thin grey/black skins intact (they add flavour) and have not been cleaned. They are vastly superior to the white ready prepared ones you can buy now. It is not at all difficult or time-consuming to clean squid.

CLEANING SQUID

To clean squid, hold the sac in one hand and pull off the head and tentacles with the other. Some of the insides will come away with the head. Cut off the tentacles just in front of the eyes. You will feel a tiny hard lump at the top of the tentacles – squeeze it out and discard it. Reserve the tentacles. Remove all the rest of the insides of the sac, including the long flexible quill, and discard. Pour running water into the sac and squeeze out anything remaining inside. Dry with kitchen paper.

Tomatoes

Even in summer it is not always possible to buy ripe tomatoes, so plan ahead and leave them to ripen in a warm light place for two to three days. Search out varieties such as Delice, Momotara and Roma that are 'grown for flavour'. When there are no decent tomatoes in the stores or market use tins of Italian plum tomatoes for sauces. The more expensive brands are usually less acidic.

SKINNING TOMATOES

Pierce the skins, immerse in boiling water for 10 seconds. Drain and remove the skins.

SUN-DRIED TOMATOES

Sun-dried tomatoes are either packed in oil or are dry and require reconstituting. Quantities in the recipes refer to those packed in oil.

To reconstitute dry tomatoes: cover with a mixture of one-third cider or mild white wine vinegar to two-thirds boiling water. Leave to soak for 1 hour, then turn them over and leave for a further hour. Drain, then pat dry on kitchen paper. Pack in jars and cover in olive oil.

TOMATO CONCASSÉ

Skin, halve and remove the seeds with your fingers. Cut the tomato flesh into neat dice.

ESSENTIALS

Chicken Stock

Stock will always have better flavour when made from fresh chicken, either inexpensive joints such as necks and wings or the carcasses from boned chicken. A whole fowl can also be used and then served cold. Alternatively, you can use bones and scraps from cooked chicken or a mixture of cooked and fresh.

1.25–1.75 kg/3–4 lb chicken carcasses, joints and scraps, uncooked or cooked	2 carrots, coarsely chopped
	1 stalk of celery with leaves, coarsely chopped
1 teaspoon salt	bouquet garni
1 unpeeled onion, quartered	6 crushed peppercorns

Place the chicken in a large saucepan and cover with cold water. Add the salt and slowly bring to a boil. Skim off any grey scum that rises to the surface in the first few minutes of simmering. Add the vegetables and flavourings. Cover and simmer for 2 to 3 hours. If you are using a whole chicken, remove it after $1\frac{1}{2}$ hours. Strain the stock and taste; if the flavour is too weak, boil until reduced. Cool, then refrigerate. Skim off the fat when it has congealed. Any remaining fat can be removed when the stock is reheated by drawing a piece of kitchen paper over the surface. Stock freezes well but needs to be boiled for 5 minutes every second day if it is kept in the refrigerator.

Fish Stock

1 kg/2 lb white fish bones
and trimmings
75 g/3 oz mixture of onion,
white part of leek, celery
and fennel bulb, finely
chopped
1 tablespoon extra virgin
olive oil

1.2 L/2 pt water
splash of dry white wine
(optional)
salt and freshly ground
black pepper

Wash the fish bones and chop. Sauté the vegetables in the oil, stirring, until softened. Add the fish, water and wine. Simmer for 20 minutes, skimming when necessary. Strain through a fine or muslin-lined sieve. Season with salt and pepper.

Anchoïade

MAKES APPROX 50 g/2 oz

2–4 cloves garlic
20 anchovy fillets
1 tablespoon lemon juice
8 tablespoons extra virgin
olive oil

freshly ground black
pepper

In a small food processor bowl, blend all the ingredients together, adding extra olive oil if necessary. It will keep for 10 days in the refrigerator.

Béchamel Sauce

MAKES 300 ml/ ½ pt

25 g/1 oz butter
1 ½ tablespoons flour
300 ml/ ½ pt cold milk
salt and freshly ground
   black pepper

½ bay leaf or freshly grated
   nutmeg

Melt the butter in a small pan and stir in the flour. Cook gently over low heat for 1 minute. Gradually pour in the milk a little at a time, stirring continually. Season with salt and pepper and add the bay leaf or nutmeg. Still stirring, bring the sauce to the boil, turn down the heat and simmer for 5 minutes until it has thickened. Season to taste with salt and pepper.

If you are not planning to use the béchamel immediately, allow it to cool slightly, then gently wipe a knob of butter over the surface to prevent a skin from forming.

Mustard and Sun-dried Tomato Sauce

A pungent but light sauce that will add dash to grilled fish, rabbit, chicken or sautéd chicken livers.

MAKES ABOUT 300 ml/ ½ pt – ENOUGH FOR 6–8 SERVINGS

25 g/1 oz butter
1 shallot, finely chopped
1 tablespoon flour
1–2 tablespoons Dijon
   mustard
300 ml/ ½ pt chicken stock

salt and freshly ground
   black pepper
50 g/2 oz sun-dried
   tomatoes, chopped
1 tablespoon chopped
   parsley

Heat the butter in a saucepan and soften the shallot.

Add the flour, cook for 1 minute, then stir in the mustard. Slowly pour in the stock, stirring all the time, and simmer for 2 minutes.

Season with salt and pepper. Stir in the sun-dried tomatoes and heat through. Add the parsley just before serving.

Pesto

This is a most wonderful and useful sauce. Its affinity with pasta is well known but it will also pep up rice dishes, stuffings and soups. The flavour is very concentrated so use it in small amounts.

MAKES 300 ml/SCANT ½ pt

4 cloves garlic, chopped
125 g/4 oz fresh basil
   leaves
125 ml/4 fl oz extra virgin
   olive oil

50 g/2 oz toasted pine nuts
75 g/3 oz grated Parmesan
   cheese
salt and freshly ground
   black pepper

Put the garlic and basil leaves in the food processor bowl and turn the machine on. Slowly add about half the oil until it makes a smooth purée. Add the pine nuts and a little more oil, followed by the cheese and the remaining oil – do not over-process. Season with salt and pepper.

Allow to rest for at least 1 hour before use. Any surplus can be kept in a sealed jar in the fridge.

To freeze: Purée the basil, oil, nuts and salt. Freeze. Add the garlic and cheese when thawed before use.

Red Pesto

Add 50 g/2 oz sun-dried tomatoes to the mixture instead of the pine nuts.

Red Pepper Sauce

MAKES 450 ml/¾ pt MEDIUM-THICK SAUCE

4 tablespoons extra virgin
  olive oil
2 red peppers, grilled,
  skinned, seeded and
  liquidized

500 g/1 lb ripe tomatoes,
  skinned, seeded and
  liquidized
1 clove garlic, crushed
salt and freshly ground
  black pepper

Using the above ingredients, cook as for Tomato Sauce (page 12), adding the peppers at the same time as the tomatoes.

Tapenade

Use on bruschetta or with grilled fish or poultry.

MAKES APPROX 175 g/6 oz

125 g/4 oz pitted Kalamata
  olives
1 tablespoon Dijon mustard
1 tin of anchovies or
  10 anchovy fillets
1 tablespoon capers
2 cloves garlic, crushed

juice of ½ lemon
6 tablespoons extra virgin
  olive oil
2 tablespoons fresh basil,
  finely chopped
freshly ground black
  pepper

Place the olives in the bowl of a food processor and, with the machine running, add the mustard, anchovy fillets, capers, garlic, lemon juice and olive oil in quick succession – do not over-process, the mixture should remain grainy. Pour into a bowl, stir in the basil and season with pepper. Covered and refrigerated it will keep for 10 days.

Tomato Sauce

MAKES 900 ml/1½ pt OF SLIGHTLY THICKENED SAUCE

4 tablespoons extra virgin
  olive oil
1.25 kg/2½ lb ripe tomatoes
  with stalks, washed and
  quartered

2 cloves garlic, crushed
1 pinch of sugar
salt and freshly ground
  black pepper

Heat the oil in a large saucepan, warm for a few seconds and then add the tomatoes and garlic. Simmer gently, uncovered, until the sauce has thickened, about 20 minutes. Sieve through a vegetable *mouli*. Season with sugar and salt and pepper. If a thicker sauce is needed, simmer until reduced further.

Flavoured Butters

Flavoured butters are an easy way of adding a little dash to grilled meats and fish or plain cooked vegetables and grains. Once the flavouring is blended with the butter, roll it into a tube and wrap it in plastic or foil. Freeze until required, then just slice off what you need.

Coriander, Lime and Ginger Butter

Mix 125 g/4 oz softened butter with 2 tablespoons chopped coriander, the juice of ½ lime and 1 teaspoon freshly grated ginger root using fork or food processor. Season with salt and pepper.

HOT CORIANDER BUTTER
Substitute ½ chopped chilli pepper for the ginger in the above recipe.

Garlic Butter

Mix 125 g/4 oz softened butter with 2 crushed cloves garlic and 1 tablespoon chopped parsley either using a fork or in a food processor. Season with salt and pepper.

Herb Butters

Blend 125 g/4 oz softened butter and 2 tablespoons of any mixture of parsley, chives, tarragon, chervil, coriander, marjoram, etc., with salt and pepper.

Nasturtium Butter

20 nasturtium flowers
6 small nasturtium leaves
125 g/4 oz softened butter

salt and freshly ground
black pepper

Place the nasturtium flowers and leaves in the small bowl of a food processor. Whiz briefly, then add the butter and a little salt and pepper. Chill for at least 1 hour before use to allow the flavours to blend.

Olive Butter

Use a fork to mix 2 tablespoons finely chopped Kalamata olives and 1 clove garlic into 125 g/4 oz softened butter. Check the seasoning; if the olives are very salty, only pepper will be needed.

Smoked Salmon Butter

To 125 g/4 oz softened butter add 125 g/4 oz smoked salmon pieces and a pinch of mace and blend. Season with black pepper. With the machine running, slowly pour in the juice of ½ lemon followed by the grated lemon zest.

Tarragon Butter

Add 2 tablespoons roughly chopped tarragon to 125 g/4 oz softened butter and blend. Season with salt and pepper.

Mayonnaise

The small bowls that are now available for food processors are ideal for making mayonnaise because the blades will be covered by the eggs and properly whisked while the oil is added.

If you are using only egg yolks, be careful to add the oil very slowly as it is quick to curdle. If it should curdle, tip it into a bowl, break another egg or egg yolk into the cleaned bowl and, with the machine running, slowly pour back the curdled mixture and continue.

Whole eggs make a thinner mayonnaise that is less rich and the oil emulsifies more easily.

Basic Mayonnaise

MAKES 350 ml/12 fl oz

2 egg yolks or 2 whole eggs
   that have been kept at
   room temperature
1 teaspoon Dijon mustard
2 tablespoons white wine or
   cider vinegar or 1
   tablespoon lemon juice

salt and freshly ground
   black pepper
300 ml/ $\frac{1}{2}$ pt extra virgin
   olive oil

Place the egg yolks or whole eggs in the bowl of a food processor. Add the mustard, half of the vinegar or lemon juice, salt and pepper. Blend and, with the machine running, start pouring in the oil a few drops at a time to begin with. When the first 60 ml/2 fl oz have emulsified, the oil can be poured in a little faster but pause regularly and check the mixture for curdling.

When all the oil has been used up, add the remaining vinegar or lemon juice. Chill in a covered jar.

Aïoli

Aïoli or garlic mayonnaise is made in the same way as the basic, substituting 2–4 crushed garlic cloves for the mustard.

Curry Mayonnaise for Cold Chicken or Fish

Stir 1 teaspoon curry powder into the mayonnaise, leave for 30 minutes for the flavour to develop, taste and add more curry powder if necessary.

Green Mayonnaise for Fish

Wilt 2 generous handfuls of sorrel, washed and stalks removed, in a pan over a moderate heat or blanch two handfuls of watercress or parsley, also with stalks removed, in boiling salted water for 30 seconds. Drain and squeeze out the water. Mash or liquidize. Stir the purée into 350 ml/12 fl oz mayonnaise.

Rouille for Fish Soup or Stew

Omit the mustard and vinegar from the basic mayonnaise and instead add 2 little dried hot red chilli peppers finely chopped, $\frac{1}{4}$ teaspoon powdered saffron and 2 crushed cloves garlic.

Vinaigrette

There is a wide variety of vinegars to choose from: Champagne, sherry, wine (red or white), raspberry, cider and balsamic from Modena. These vinegars can range enormously in quality so it is a good idea to go easy on them before you have learned their true strength.

MAKES APPROX 125 ml/4 fl oz

2 tablespoons cider or wine vinegar *or* 1 tablespoon lemon juice
1 teaspoon Dijon mustard
½ teaspoon caster sugar (optional)

salt and freshly ground black pepper
90 ml/3 fl oz extra virgin olive oil or a mixture of olive and nut oil

Whisk together the vinegar, mustard and sugar, if you are using it. Add salt and pepper. Gradually whisk in the oil.

Caper vinaigrette

Add 1 tablespoon finely chopped capers.

Garlic Vinaigrette

Add 1 crushed clove garlic.

Mixed flowers and herbs vinaigrette

Add chopped nasturtium and borage flowers with chopped parsley and coriander.

Mixed herbs vinaigrette

Add 1 tablespoon finely chopped parsley, chives, chervil, tarragon, etc.

Sun-dried Tomato Vinaigrette

Add 25 g/1 oz finely chopped sun-dried tomatoes.

Yoghurt Dressing

150 ml/ ¼ pt natural yoghurt
60 ml/2 fl oz extra virgin
    olive oil
1 clove garlic, crushed

lemon juice to taste
salt and freshly ground
    black pepper

Mix all the ingredients together. Serve with crunchy salads.

For a richer dressing use a mixture of crème fraîche or fromage frais with the yoghurt.

Olive Oil Pastry

QUANTITY SUFFICIENT FOR A 23–25 cm/9–10 in TART TIN

275 g/9 oz plain flour
½ teaspoon salt
7 tablespoons extra virgin
    olive oil

1 tablespoon water
2 cloves garlic, crushed

Mix the flour and salt together in a bowl.

Heat the olive oil, water and garlic in a small saucepan until it bubbles. Stir the hot liquid into the flour to make a crumbly dough.

Press the dough evenly up the sides of the tart tin, then cover the base with the remainder.

Chill the pastry case for 1 hour before cooking.

Puff Pastry

MAKES 250 g/8 OZ PASTRY

250 g/8 oz butter
250 g/8 oz strong flour,
   plus extra

1 teaspoon salt
Scant 150 ml/¼ pt cold
   water

Melt 2 tablespoons of the butter. Sift the flour on to a cold surface such as marble, Formica or stainless steel. Add the salt and make a well in the centre. Add the water and the melted butter. Gradually work in the flour to form a soft dough, adding more water if necessary. Wrap in cling film and chill for 15 minutes.

Lightly flour the dough and roll it out into a 30 cm/12 in square. Flour the remaining butter and hit it with a rolling pin to soften. It should be about the same consistency as the dough. Shape it into a 15 cm/6 in square.

Set the butter square at an angle on the dough square so that you have four exposed triangles of dough. Fold these over to cover the butter and form an envelope. Flour the surface and turn over, seam-side down. Roll out to a rectangle 50 × 20 cm/20 × 8 in. Fold the rectangle into three, as if folding a business letter. Turn the dough 90° clockwise – this is called a 'turn'. Roll out again and fold in three, making a second turn. The turns are layering the butter between the flour. This will make the pastry puff and be meltingly light when it is baked. Wrap in cling film and refrigerate for 30 minutes. Make a note of the time and how many turns you have done. Make two more turns and refrigerate for 30 minutes. Repeat again, making a total of six turns. Chill at least 30 minutes before using.

The dough can be frozen or kept tightly wrapped in cling film in the refrigerator for four days.

Shortcrust Pastry

QUANTITY SUFFICIENT FOR A 23–25 cm/9–10 in TART TIN

200 g/7 oz plain flour
½ teaspoon salt
125 g/4 oz cold butter cut
  into 1 cm/½ in cubes

4 tablespoons cold water,
  more if necessary

METHOD 1

Put the flour and salt into the bowl of a food processor. Turn on the machine and immediately add the butter. Do not over-process or the butter will become too soft – 5 seconds should be sufficient. With the machine running, add the water and in about a further 5 seconds a ball of dough should have formed – turn the machine off immediately. If the dough is still separate, add another ½ table-spoon of cold water. Wrap the pastry in cling film and chill for 30 minutes.

METHOD 2

Sift the flour and salt into a bowl. Rub in the butter cubes with your fingertips. Make a well in the centre of the mixture and pour in the water. Mix quickly with a knife to form crumbs (add a little more water if necessary) and press the dough into a ball. Wrap in cling film and chill for 30 minutes.

TO BAKE BLIND

Heat the oven to 190°C/375°F/Gas Mark 5. Lightly butter the tart tin. Roll out the dough; line the tin and chill until firm. Prick the bottom with a fork. Cut a circle of greaseproof paper or baking parchment about 5 cm/2 in larger than the tin. Lay it on the pastry and fill it in an even layer with dried beans or ceramic baking balls. Bake for 15 minutes; remove the paper and weights and return the pastry to the oven for a further 5 minutes.

Sweet Shortcrust Pastry

QUANTITY SUFFICIENT FOR A 23–25 cm/9–10 in TART TIN

175 g/6 oz plain flour
½ teaspoon salt
65 g/2½ oz caster sugar

100 g/3½ oz cold unsalted
  butter, cut into cubes
4 tablespoons water or 3
  egg yolks

METHOD 1
Put the flour, salt and sugar into the bowl of a food processor. Then follow the directions for Shortcrust Pastry, above.

METHOD 2
Sift the flour and salt into a bowl and add the sugar. Continue as for the Shortcrust Pastry, above.

Olive Oil Bread

This lovely olive oil bread is so good on its own that you will never feel the need to butter it. It goes well with savoury food but, as you might guess, it isn't that good spread with jam. The more time the dough has to rise the less yeast you need and the better the texture and taste of the bread will be. If you have the time to leave the dough overnight in a cool place, decrease the yeast by one-third.

MAKES 1 LOAF

15 g/½ oz fresh yeast or 1½
  teaspoons dried yeast
275 m/9 fl oz lukewarm
  water
2 teaspoons salt

500 g/1 lb unbleached
  strong white flour
4 tablespoons extra virgin
  olive oil

Dissolve the yeast in the warm water. (If you are using easy-blend yeast omit this step.) Mix the salt into the flour, make a well in the centre and add the yeasty water and the olive oil. Knead until the dough is smooth and elastic. This can also be done in a food processor. Place the dough in a bowl, cover with a plastic bag fitted over the rim, and leave to rise in a warm place until doubled in volume, at least 3 hours or longer.

Knock the dough down and knead it again, form it into a ball, and place on an oiled baking sheet or pizza tin. Cover with a large ovenproof earthenware or Pyrex bowl. A large earthenware flower-pot can also be used but check that it will fit into the oven. This will create a mini-oven that will delay the crust forming on the bread and give the crumb a chance to expand. Leave the dough to rise again for about 1 hour.

Preheat the oven to 220°C/425°F/Gas Mark 7.

Five minutes before you intend to bake the loaf, lift off the bowl, gently reshape the loaf, which will have spread out, re-cover and place in the oven.

Bake the loaf for 30 minutes. Using oven gloves, remove the baking sheet with the bread and bowl. Lift the bowl off with the help of a spatula and the oven gloves. Return the bread to the oven, uncovered, for another 10 minutes or until a good crust has formed. Place on a rack to cool.

VARIATIONS
Add 1 heaped tablespoon of sun-dried tomato purée and 6 chopped sun-dried tomatoes after the first rise. Omit the salt as the purée is very salty.

Add a small handful of black olives, stoned and chopped, after the first rise.

Add about 8 small chopped sage leaves after the first rise.

Add 2 teaspoons of rosemary leaves after the first rise.

Ciabatta

Add about 4–5 tablespoons more water to the Olive Oil Bread to make a very soft dough. Let it rise without kneading, then form into two cylindrical flat shapes, adding just enough flour to achieve this. Place on an oiled baking sheet and cover with an ovenproof bowl or ceramic flowerpot. After it has risen again, bake as for the Olive Oil Bread. Remove the cover and return to the oven for 5 minutes to form a crust.

Polenta

Polenta is cornmeal, which is a popular grain in Italy and used in America for baking breads and muffins. If you are using quick-cooking polenta, follow the directions on the packet and adjust the quantities. It isn't as good as the old-fashioned grain but it is still worth using if you can't locate the authentic sort. We have only used grilled polenta in this book, but it can also be used wet – with cheese and butter stirred into it when cooked and served hot with a mushroom or creamy sauce.

SERVES 8–10

1.75 L/3 pt water   350 g/12 oz polenta
1 teaspoon salt

Bring the water to the boil in a large saucepan, add the salt and turn the heat down until it is just simmering. Take a handful of polenta and let it trickle through your fingers into the water in a fine stream, stirring with a wooden spoon until completely blended. Or pour the polenta slowly from a jug. Cook for about 25 minutes, stirring until the polenta comes away from the sides of the saucepan and is very stiff.

Pour the polenta on to a wooden block or chopping board and spread out to form a layer 2 cm/¾ in thick. Leave to cool completely,** then cut into wedges or slices for grilling.

Note: There will be a thick layer of polenta left sticking to the pan. Leave it to soak in cold water for 1 hour and it will then lift off easily.

** *Can be prepared in advance up to this point.*

SOUPS

Black Bean Soup

Black beans have a delicious, almost meaty flavour and make excellent soup and salads. Go for the smaller variety. They are sometimes labelled turtle beans and have the best flavour. Health food stores usually stock them. The soup looks very appetizing, particularly with a dab of soured cream swirled into its rich darkness.

SERVES 6

250 g/8 oz black beans
1 onion, chopped
1 clove garlic, finely
    chopped
1 carrot, finely chopped
1 stalk celery, finely
    chopped
½ teaspoon ground
    coriander
2 teaspoons cumin seeds
3 tablespoons extra virgin
    olive oil

400 g/14 oz tin chopped
    tomatoes
4–6 tablespoons chopped
    coriander leaves
1–2 chilli peppers, seeded
    and finely chopped
1.2 L/2pt vegetable stock
salt and freshly ground
    black pepper
6 tablespoons sour cream,
    to serve

Either soak the beans overnight in water or cover with boiling water and leave for 3–4 hours. Drain, rinse and drain again.

Sweat the onion, garlic, carrot, celery, coriander and cumin seeds in the oil for a few minutes. Stir in the beans, tomatoes, half the chopped coriander, chillies and stock. Simmer until the beans are tender, about 3 hours. Season with salt and pepper.**

Process if you want a smooth soup or serve as is garnished with sour cream and coriander.

** *Can be prepared in advance up to this point.*

Carrot, Orange and Coriander Soup

Fresh coriander is now usually available in supermarkets and although you can use the ground coriander instead, make sure it is still fresh as once opened it quickly loses its flavour.

SERVES 6

1 medium onion, chopped
50 g/2 oz butter
½ teaspoon ground
   coriander or 1 tablespoon
   chopped coriander
500 g/1 lb carrots, diced
900 ml/1 ½ pt chicken stock

grated rind and juice of 1
   large orange
salt and freshly ground
   black pepper
6 teaspoons crème fraîche
   or Greek yoghurt, to
   serve

Cook the onion in the butter until it is soft but not coloured. If you are using ground coriander sprinkle it over the onions and then add the carrots. Stir until the butter has been absorbed. Pour in the stock and simmer until the carrots are soft. Remove from the heat and cool slightly.

Liquidize the mixture until it is very smooth, add the chopped coriander, if you are using it, orange juice and rind. Season with salt and pepper.**

Serve either hot with crème fraîche or cold with yoghurt.

** *Can be prepared in advance up to this point.*

Celeriac Soup with Garlic Croûtons

Celeriac makes a smooth creamy soup with only a modicum of cream. It is delicious with garlic croûtons to give it added flavour and crunch.

SERVES 6

1 medium onion, chopped
50 g/2 oz butter
1 medium celeriac, diced
900 ml/1 ½ pt chicken stock
salt and freshly ground
    black pepper
4 tablespoons double cream

For the croûtons:
extra virgin olive oil
1 clove garlic, sliced
3 slices dryish bread, cut
    into 1-cm/½-in squares

Cook the onion in butter until it is soft but not coloured. Add the celeriac and stir until the butter has been absorbed. Pour in the stock and simmer until the celeriac is cooked. Remove from the heat and allow to cool slightly. Season with salt and pepper. Liquidize until very smooth and stir in the cream.**

To make the croûtons: heat some olive oil in a frying pan and add the garlic. Fry the croûtons until they are golden, turning them frequently. Discard the garlic and drain the croûtons on kitchen paper.

Reheat the soup but do not let it boil. Serve the croûtons separately.

** *Can be prepared in advance up to this point.*

Fennel and Celeriac Soup

Fennel and celeriac combine beautifully in soup. The celeriac gives the soup a creamy texture and the fennel adds a subtle flavour. It is good enough for grand occasions.

SERVES 8

1 tablespoon extra virgin
   olive oil
15 g / ½ oz butter
1 large mild Spanish onion,
   chopped
1 celeriac, weighing about
   625 g / 1 ¼ lb

2 fennel bulbs
salt and freshly ground
   black pepper
600 ml / 1 pt chicken stock
600 ml / 1 pt water
finely chopped chervil or
   parsley, to serve

Heat the oil and butter in a large saucepan, stir in the onion and cook over a gentle heat, stirring occasionally, until it is translucent.

While the onion is cooking, peel and cube the celeriac. Using a vegetable peeler, peel the outer coarse stalks of the fennel bulbs. Slice all the stalks and some of the feathery leaves. Add both vegetables and some salt and pepper to the pan and stir for a minute or two.

Add the stock and water, cover and simmer for 25 minutes, or until the vegetables are tender.

Purée the soup in a blender, return to the pan and adjust the seasoning.** Serve hot, garnished with the chervil or parsley.

** *Can be prepared in advance up to this point.*

Puy Lentil and Cumin Soup

The slate-green lentils from Le Puy in the south-west of France have a rich spiciness that makes them the most delicious lentil of all. They go particularly well with cumin.

SERVES 6–8

1 medium onion, chopped
3 tablespoons extra virgin
    olive oil
250 g/8 oz Puy lentils,
    rinsed well
1 clove garlic, crushed
1 teaspoon ground cumin

1.2 L/2 pt chicken stock
salt and freshly ground
    black pepper
1 tablespoon chopped
    coriander or parsley, to
    serve

Cook the onion in the oil until it is soft but not coloured. Stir in the lentils, garlic and cumin. Add the stock and simmer for 30–40 minutes until the lentils are soft. Season well with salt and pepper. Remove from the heat and cool slightly.

Liquidize briefly, leaving some of the lentils whole, and thin with extra stock if necessary.**

Reheat and sprinkle with the coriander or parsley before serving.

** *Can be prepared in advance up to this point.*

Red Pepper and Carrot Soup

SERVES 4

1 medium onion, chopped
25 g/1 oz butter
350 g/12 oz carrots, sliced
1.2 L/2 pt chicken stock
2 red peppers, grilled,
    peeled (page 5), seeded
    and chopped

salt and freshly ground
    black pepper
6 teaspoons Greek yoghurt,
    to serve

Cook the onion in the butter until it is soft, add the carrots and stir until the butter is absorbed. Pour in the stock and simmer, covered, until the carrots are cooked. Liquidize with the peppers.** Season well and serve either hot or cold with a spoonful of yoghurt in each bowl.

** *Can be prepared in advance up to this point.*

Sorrel Soup

Unless you grow your own sorrel – or have a generous friend who does – it can be difficult to obtain in this country. Should you have a spare corner of your garden though, two sorrel plants will give an ample supply, from early summer right through to the hard frosts. This soup can also be made with a mixture of 250 g/8 oz spinach and a handful of sorrel. Add a squeeze of lemon juice to the chicken stock and mix the sorrel when you purée the soup.

SERVES 6

1 medium onion, chopped
50 g/2 oz butter
2 medium potatoes, peeled and diced
3 generous handfuls of sorrel leaves, washed and destalked
900 ml/1 ½ pt chicken stock

¼ grated nutmeg
salt and freshly ground black pepper
3–4 tablespoons double cream
1 small bunch of chives, to serve

Cook the onion in butter until it is soft but not coloured. Add the potatoes and stir together until the butter has been absorbed. Take half the sorrel and warm it through with the mixture until it becomes limp. Pour in the stock and simmer until the potatoes are cooked. Grate in a little nutmeg, season with salt and pepper and remove from the heat. Leave to cool completely. Pour into the bowl of a food processor and add the remaining sorrel. Whiz until the the uncooked sorrel is speckly. Stir in the cream.**

Reheat gently until hot but do not allow it to boil or the uncooked sorrel will lose its colour. Sprinkle with chives and serve.

** *Can be prepared in advance up to this point.*

Spinach and Horseradish Soup

Horseradish gives this soup a distinctive bite – add it a little at a
time so as not to swamp the flavour of the spinach.

SERVES 6

1 medium onion, chopped	salt and freshly ground
50 g/2 oz butter	pepper
1 kg/2 lb spinach, washed	2 tablespoons creamed
and stalks removed	horseradish
1 teaspoon flour	6 teaspoons natural
900 ml/1 ½ pt chicken stock	yoghurt, to serve

Cook the onion in butter until it is soft but not coloured, then add
the spinach and heat it gently until it becomes limp. Stir in the
flour, heat through and pour in the chicken stock. Boil for 1 minute
and remove from the heat. Leave to cool slightly.

Season with salt and pepper and liquidize until very smooth. Stir in
the creamed horseradish to taste.**

Reheat and serve with a teaspoon of natural yoghurt in each bowl.

** *Can be prepared in advance up to this point.*

Squash Soup with Chervil

There are many kinds of winter squash available and among the best are butternut and acorn. They have good texture and flavour and make a soup similar but superior to pumpkin.

SERVES 4–6

1 butternut squash	salt and freshly ground
1 acorn squash	black pepper
1 medium onion, sliced	60 ml/2 fl oz cream or
50 g/2 oz butter	crème fraîche
½ teaspoon ground mace	1 tablespoon chopped
900 ml/1½ pt chicken stock	chervil, to serve

Preheat the oven to 200°C/400°F/Gas Mark 6.

Halve the squash, remove the seeds and place them on an oiled baking tray with the cut sides down. Bake for 45–60 minutes until tender – the different varieties will not necessarily require the same amount of cooking time.

Cook the onion in butter until it is soft but not coloured, scoop the flesh from the squash halves and add it to the pan. Sprinkle on the mace and stir in the stock. Simmer for 2 minutes, remove from the heat and allow to cool slightly. Season with salt and pepper and liquidize until smooth. Stir in the cream or crème fraîche.**

Reheat gently and sprinkle with chervil.

** *Can be prepared in advance up to this point.*

Cold Fresh Tomato Soup

An onion soaked overnight in milk softens its bite and makes it more digestible – a good tip to follow when onion is used uncooked as in this soup. If the tomatoes lack flavour, stir in a pinch of medium-strength curry powder at the same time as the other seasonings.

SERVES 4

1 small onion, soaked
    overnight in milk
1 kg/2 lb ripe tomatoes,
    skinned and seeded
1 teaspoon caster sugar

salt and freshly ground
    black pepper
150 ml/¼ pt single cream
1 small bunch of chives, to
    serve

Drain the onion and discard the milk.

Liquidize the tomatoes and the roughly chopped onion until you have a smooth mixture, then pour it into a bowl. Season with the sugar, salt and pepper. Add just enough cream to soften the flavour of the tomatoes without overwhelming it.

Chill for at least 4 hours.** Scatter the chives on top of the soup before serving.

** *Can be prepared in advance up to this point.*

Jellied Tomato and Basil Soup

A refreshing soup for a hot summer's evening, but only worth making with really ripe good-flavoured tomatoes such as Delice or Roma. Prepare the soup 12–24 hours in advance.

SERVES 6

1.5 kg/3 1b ripe tomatoes
3 cloves garlic, crushed
150 ml/¼ pt dry white wine
15 g/½ oz caster sugar
salt and freshly ground
   black pepper
15 g/½ oz powdered or leaf
   gelatine

12–16 fresh basil leaves,
   chopped

To serve:
6 teaspoons natural yoghurt
   or crème fraîche
6 small basil leaves

Pierce the tomato skins and place them in a large saucepan with the garlic, 90 ml/3 fl oz of the wine, sugar, salt and pepper. Bring gently to the boil and simmer for 10 minutes. Leave to cool. Turn into a blender and whiz to a purée. Push through a fine sieve to remove the seeds and skin.

Soak the gelatine (snip the leaves into small pieces) in the remaining 60 ml/2 fl oz of wine for 3 minutes, then dissolve it over a gentle heat – do not allow it to boil. Pour the gelatine into the tomato mixture and check the seasoning. Stir in the basil and pour the mixture into a bowl for chilling.

Refrigerate for 12–24 hours.** Serve spooned into individual bowls with a dollop of yoghurt or crème fraîche on the ruffled surface of the jellied soup, topped with a basil leaf.

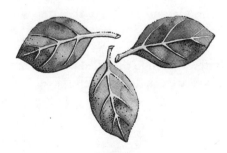

** *Can be prepared in advance up to this point.*

STARTERS

Brandade of Salt Cod

Brandade is a very addictive mixture of salt cod, milk and olive oil. With a food processor it is easy to make and produces very special and rewarding results. Salt cod needs to be soaked before it can be poached – ask your fishmonger how long to soak his particular salt cod, the time can vary between 24 and 48 hours.

SERVES 4

500 g/1 lb salt cod
125 ml/4 fl oz extra virgin olive oil
1–2 cloves garlic, crushed
125 ml/4 fl oz full cream milk
freshly ground black pepper
12 triangles of thin white bread, fried in olive oil
finely chopped parsley

Soak the salt cod for at least 24 hours, changing the water several times. Place in a large pan of cold water and bring slowly to the boil. Simmer at the lowest possible heat (the water should barely shudder) for 10–15 minutes, until the flesh is just tender. Don't overcook. Drain, remove the bones and skin and flake the fish with a fork.

Place the cod flakes in a food processor. Heat the oil and garlic in one saucepan until very hot and heat the milk until almost boiling in another. Remove the garlic and add it to the cod. With the motor running, add the hot oil and milk to the cod, in a steady slow stream, until they are completely absorbed. Season with pepper.**

Turn out on to a platter. Arrange the fried bread triangles around the edge, sprinkle the parsley over the top and serve.

** *Can be prepared in advance up to this point.*

Alternatively, the brandade can be made by adding the cod to the saucepan with the hot oil, then beating hard with a wooden spoon, over very low heat until the oil is absorbed. Beat in the milk by the tablespoon. Move the cod off the heat if it gets too hot and threatens to brown. Continue until the milk is absorbed, then season and turn the fish out on to a platter.

Note: If the brandade is too salty, add 1 or 2 boiled potatoes, mashed, and more milk. The brandade can be served cold or hot, and can be used as a savoury filling for tomatoes or peppers.

Marinated Mixed Fish with Coriander
and Chilli Sauce

The fish listed here are only suggestions: any firm well-flavoured fish will do, although a mixture of colours as well as textures is best. If you are using scallops check that they have not been frozen. Freezing ruins the texture and the delicate flavour. By doubling the quantities this dish can be served as a light main course.

SERVES 6

750/1½ lb mixed very fresh filleted monkfish, salmon and scallops
2 ripe avocados

For the marinade:
2 cloves garlic, chopped
300 ml/½ pt lime juice or a mixture of lemon and lime juice
1 pinch of cayenne pepper
salt and freshly ground black pepper

For the sauce:
65 g/2½ oz coriander leaves and smaller stems
½–1 chilli pepper, seeded and chopped
grated rind and juice from ½ lime or lemon
1 clove garlic
5–6 tablespoons extra virgin olive oil
salt and freshly ground black pepper

Using a very sharp knife, finely slice the fish into 5 mm/¼ in pieces. Slice the scallops into 3 discs, but leave the coral whole. Lay all the slices in a shallow dish. Mix a marinade of the garlic, lime juice and cayenne pepper, and pour it over the fish. Season with salt and pepper, cover and refrigerate for at least 3 hours, stirring occasionally.

To make the sauce, place the coriander and chilli into the bowl of a food processor, and blend them with the lime or lemon zest and juice and the garlic. Gradually add the olive oil and season with salt and pepper.**

Peel and slice the avocados just before serving and arrange the slices on individual plates with the drained fish. Spoon the sauce over the top.

** *Can be prepared in advance up to this point.*

Pickled Herrings with Sour Cream and Chives

Herrings are inexpensive and, marinated, make a delicious first course. Only buy them if they are really fresh and shiny – if they are limp and dull they will have lost much of their flavour and will be difficult to bone.

SERVES 4

4 medium-sized fresh
  herrings
400 ml/14 fl oz water
  mixed with 25 g/1 oz
  salt
1 bunch of fresh dill
2 medium sweet onions,
  finely sliced
150 ml/¼ pt sour cream
1 bunch of chives, chopped

For the marinade: 400 ml/14
  fl oz white wine or cider
  vinegar
125 g/4 oz sugar
1 clove garlic, sliced
1 bay leaf
6 cloves
10 black peppercorns,
  crushed
10 juniper berries, crushed
cayenne pepper

Remove the head and tail from the herrings and clean them. Split open the body and run the blade of a small knife under the larger bones to detach them from the flesh. Stand the fish on a board backbone upwards and with a rolling pin gently bang along its entire length. Turn the fish over and remove the backbone with the smaller bones still attached. Slice into 2 fillets and put them in a bowl. Cover with the salted water and leave for 3 hours. Mix all the marinade ingredients and leave them to stand, stirring occasionally, until the sugar has dissolved.

Drain the herrings and pat dry on kitchen paper. Lay the fillets on a board and place a sprig of dill and some onion slices on each one. Roll the fillets up and pack them into a container. Cover with the marinade and leave in the refrigerator for 3–5 days.**

To serve, drain the herrings and remove the old onions and dill. Either roll them up again round some fresh dill or slice them and arrange in a dish with some fresh onion rings on top. Cover with the sour cream and sprinkle with chopped chives or dill.

** *Can be prepared in advance up to this point.*

Salmon Carpaccio

The salmon for carpaccio must be very fresh. Only buy the escallops ready-sliced if you can really be sure they have only recently been prepared.

SERVES 4

4 x 50 g/2 oz escallop of
  salmon about 1-cm/
  ½-in thick
olive oil

For the relish:
1 small red pepper,
  chopped very finely
½ yellow pepper, chopped
  very finely

2 shallots, chopped very
  finely
juice of ½ lemon
125 ml/4 fl oz extra virgin
  olive oil
salt and freshly ground
  black pepper

1 tablespoon chopped dill
  leaves, to serve

Cut 8 x 20-cm/8-in squares from cling film and lightly oil one side.

Check that there are no bones left in the escallops and lay them on the oiled side of the cling film squares. Cover with the other squares – oiled side towards the fish. Using the side of a cleaver or rolling pin, gently flatten the salmon until it becomes transparent. Leave it in the fridge until just before serving.**

Mix together all the relish ingredients. Gently peel the fish from the paper and lay it on individual plates. Spoon the relish over the top and sprinkle with dill.

** *Can be prepared in advance up to this point.*

Steamed Scallops on Aubergine Slices

As long as the scallops are fresh, not frozen, this dish can be prepared with either the large king scallops or the small and much cheaper queens (allow 6 per person). If you do not have a steamer, a metal colander that fits 5–8 cm/2–3 in into a pan will do instead. Wrap a damp tea towel tightly round the part that protrudes to seal the holes and use the panlid as the cover.

SERVES 4

2 small aubergines, about 5 cm/2 in in diameter
extra virgin olive oil
salt and freshly ground black pepper

8–12 fresh scallops
fresh mint leaves, to serve

Using a sharp knife, slice the aubergines as finely as possible. Discard the outer slices, which are mostly skin. You should have about 10 slices per aubergine.

Heat a ridged cast-iron grill pan until it is very hot and, separately, bring some water to the boil in the bottom of a steamer pan.

Brush the aubergine slices with olive oil and grill both sides until they are lightly browned. Drain the cooked slices on kitchen paper, season with salt and pepper, and keep them warm while the rest are grilling. Meanwhile, season the scallops and steam them briefly; timing really is of the essence as overcooked scallops become tough – 2–3 minutes for queens and 4–5 minutes for large scallops.

Lay the aubergines on individual plates with the scallops on top. Scatter with mint leaves and serve immediately.

Spicy Aubergine and Tomato Salad

This is a most successful mixture of flavours and textures. It is also very light because the method of frying the aubergine uses very little oil.

SERVES 4

1 large very firm aubergine
1 ½ teaspoons salt
4 tablespoons extra virgin olive oil
1 large mild onion, finely chopped
¾ teaspoon ground cumin
1 teaspoon ground allspice
1 pinch of cayenne pepper
1 clove garlic, very finely chopped
5 tomatoes, skinned, seeded and cubed

2 tablespoons sultanas
salt and freshly ground black pepper

To serve:
1 small lettuce
2 tablespoons chopped fresh mint or basil
175 ml/6 fl oz plain yoghurt

Peel and cut the aubergine into 1-cm/½-in cubes. Place in a colander, mix well with the salt and leave to drain for 30 minutes.

Heat 2 tablespoons of the oil in a frying pan, add the onion, cumin, allspice, cayenne pepper and garlic. Cook, stirring occasionally, until the onions are golden. Stir in the tomatoes and sultanas and cook just to heat through, about a minute or two, then turn into a bowl.

Squeeze the aubergine cubes dry in a clean tea towel. Heat the remaining 2 tablespoons of oil in the frying pan and fry the aubergine, stirring continually, until the cubes are tender and golden, about 10 minutes. Tip into the bowl with the onions, gently mix together and leave to cool. Season to taste.**

Arrange some lettuce leaves on individual plates. Place a mound of the aubergine mixture in the centre and sprinkle with the mint or basil. Serve the yoghurt separately.

** *Can be prepared in advance up to this point.*

Avocado and Papaya Salad with Lime Vinaigrette

Slices of orange papaya and green avocado make a beautiful first course. The flavours complement each other and the lime vinaigrette gives just the right tang.

SERVES 6

For the vinaigrette:

grated rind and juice of 1 lime

¼ teaspoon salt

6 tablespoons extra virgin olive oil

6 tablespoons sunflower oil

1 pinch of sugar

3 ripe avocados

3 ripe papayas

125–150 g/4–5 oz watercress leaves

salt and freshly ground black pepper

Make the vinaigrette and season it with salt and pepper.

Halve, stone and peel the avocados. Cut into slices crosswise. Halve the papayas and remove all the black seeds. Peel off the skin and cut the flesh into crosswise slices.

Arrange slices of both papaya and avocado on six plates. Place the watercress around the edge. Season very lightly with salt and pepper and spoon some vinaigrette over the top.

Avocado, Red Pepper and Sun-dried Tomato Salad

This colourful mélange makes an attractive addition to a buffet table as well as being an easy starter.

SERVES 4

1 large red pepper, grilled, peeled (page 5), seeded and finely sliced

125 g/4 oz sun-dried tomatoes, drained and sliced

1 large or 2 small avocados

For the vinaigrette:

1 tablespoon chopped chervil

3 tablespoons extra virgin olive oil

1 tablespoon cider vinegar

salt and freshly ground black pepper

Prepare the peppers and tomatoes in advance and make the vinaigrette.**

Just before serving, slice the avocados, arrange with the peppers and tomatoes and toss with the vinaigrette.

** *Can be prepared in advance up to this point.*

Skate and Wild Rice Salad

This salad could also make a light main course; simply double the quantities and serve it with a green salad. Balsamic vinegars vary enormously in price but when you taste one of the better ones it has a smoothness and depth of flavour that merits the expense.

SERVES 4

25 g/1 oz butter
1 shallot, finely chopped
125 g/4 oz wild rice
500 g/11b skate wings
1 onion
bouquet garni
salt and freshly ground
    black pepper
200 g/7 oz fine French
    beans, blanched in salted
    water for 2 minutes and
    cut into 2.5 cm/1 in
    lengths

1 red pepper, grilled, peeled
    (page 5), seeded and
    finely sliced
2 tablespoons capers
2 tablespoons chopped
    parsley

For the vinaigrette:
pared rind of ½ lemon or
    lime, finely chopped
4 tablespoons extra virgin
    olive oil
1 tablespoon balsamic
    vinegar

Melt the butter in a medium-sized saucepan and soften the shallot. Stir in the rice and pour in enough water barely to cover it. Simmer, covered, for 25 minutes, checking regularly and topping up with water when necessary. Season with salt towards the end of the cooking time.

Gently poach the skate with an onion, bouquet garni, salt and pepper for 5 minutes. Drain and set it aside to cool, then remove the flesh from the bone in long strips.

Mix the beans, pepper, capers and parsley into the wild rice, then gently fold in the skate. Season with salt and pepper.** Add the chopped lemon or lime rind to the olive oil and balsamic vinegar, season, and pour over the salad just before serving.

** *Can be prepared in advance up to this point.*

Salad of Grilled Squid and Spinach Leaves

Squid are tender and sweet when grilled very briefly. Combined with peppers and spinach leaves they make an attractive, healthy and special salad. Serve either as a starter or in increased quantities as a light main course.

SERVES 4

125 g/4 oz baby spinach leaves, washed and stalks removed
50 g/2 oz rocket leaves, washed
1 red pepper, grilled, peeled (page 5), seeded and finely sliced

8 x 10 cm/4 in squid, cleaned (page 5)
extra virgin olive oil
salt and freshly ground black pepper
juice of ½ lemon

Arrange a small mound of the salad leaves on individual plates with half of the pepper slices on the top.**

Cut the squid sacs open and slice each one into four strips. Leave the tentacles whole.

Heat a ridged cast-iron grill pan or large heavy-bottomed frying pan until very hot.

Brush the strips of squid and the tentacles lightly with olive oil and season with salt and pepper. Grill rapidly for 30 seconds on each side. Remove from the pan and drain on kitchen paper. Lay the fish on the salad with the remaining pepper slices. Squeeze a little lemon juice over each plate and drizzle with more olive oil. Season with salt and pepper. Serve immediately while the squid is still hot.

** Can be prepared in advance up to this point.

Watercress, Chicory and Orange Salad
with Sunflower Seeds

This is a salad of contrasts – bitter chicory, sweet orange and crunchy sunflower seeds.

SERVES 4

50 g/2 oz sunflower seeds
1 tablespoon extra virgin
    olive oil
2 bunches of watercress
1 large navel orange

3 heads of chicory
Vinaigrette made with
    balsamic vinegar (page
    16)

Fry the sunflower seeds in the olive oil until they are lightly coloured. Drain on kitchen paper.

Wash and dry the watercress and remove the coarse stems.

With a sharp knife cut away the outer skin and white pith from the orange. Then cut out the sections of orange flesh, leaving behind the membrane.**

Just before serving slice the chicory and mix it in with the watercress and orange. Toss the salad with the vinaigrette and turn into a serving dish. Scatter with the sunflower seeds.

** *Can be prepared in advance up to this point.*

Bruschetta

At its simplest bruschetta is a slice of good crusty bread that has been grilled, rubbed with a clove of garlic, seasoned, then drizzled with olive oil. Try it with a fragrant oil such as De la Vallée des Baux or lemony Colonna Granverde. It is the perfect accompaniment to many starters. If served with a topping, bruschetta can be a starter or a light main meal. All of the following toppings can be made in advance and spread just before serving.

Bruschetta with Anchoïade**

Make the bruschetta, spread with Anchoïade (page 8) and dot with olives and capers.

Bruschetta with Aubergine Purée and Walnuts**

Whiz 175 g/6 oz walnuts in a processor until ground. Bake 2 aubergines in a hot oven (about 220°C/425°F/Gas Mark 7), until soft, roughly 35 minutes. Cut them in half, scoop out the flesh, put it in a processor and purée with 1–2 crushed cloves garlic. Beat in the ground walnuts, 6 tablespoons extra virgin olive oil, Tabasco and salt and pepper. Make the bruschetta and spread with the purée.

Bruschetta with Bean Purée and Harissa**

400 g/14 oz can of haricot beans, drained, 2 crushed cloves garlic, 2 tablespoons extra virgin olive oil, 3 tablespoons tahini paste, ¼–1 teaspoon harissa sauce, lemon juice, salt and pepper. Blend the beans, garlic, oil and tahini together. Season with the harissa, lemon juice and salt and pepper. Make the bruschetta and spread with the purée.

*** Can be prepared in advance.*

Bruschetta with Pesto**

Make the bruschetta, spread with Pesto (page 10) and top with fine slices of grilled aubergine and slivers of sun-dried tomato.

Bruschetta with Red Pesto**

Make the bruschetta, spread with Red Pesto (page 10), a layer of Tomato Concassé (page 6) and crumbled Feta cheese.

Bruschetta with Tapenade**

Make the bruschetta, spread with Tapenade (page 11) and sprinkle with finely chopped sweet onions.

*** Can be prepared in advance.*

Puff Pastry Mini Pizzas

Tomato and Anchovy

You can make these mini pizzas in the normal round shape or if you have individual 12-cm/4½-in tart tins you can use those. If the pastry is rolled out and the tomatoes prepared well ahead of time, it is very quick to arrange the filling and pop them in the oven for a tasty and manageable first course.

SERVES 4

250 g/8 oz Puff Pastry, either home-made (page 18) or bought
8 ripe plum tomatoes, skinned, seeded and sliced

salt and freshly ground black pepper
1 tin of anchovy fillets, drained
extra virgin olive oil

Roll out the pastry until it is about 3 mm/⅛ in thick. Using a 15 cm/6 in saucepan lid, cut out four circles. Chill for 30 minutes.**

Place a baking sheet in the oven and preheat to 220°C/425°F/Gas Mark 7.

Arrange the tomato rings on the pastry in an overlapping spiral and season with salt and pepper. Lay the anchovy fillets on top of the tomatoes and drizzle on a little olive oil.

Slide the mini pizzas on to the hot baking sheet and cook for 15 minutes. Sprinkle with a little more oil before serving.

Two other delicious toppings for the mini pizzas are onion purée and Kalamata olives and grilled peppers and chèvre. The quantity and method for the pastry and baking is exactly as for the tomato and anchovy recipe (above).

** *Can be prepared in advance up to this point.*

Onion Purée and Kalamata Olives

3 tablespoons extra virgin
   olive oil plus extra to
   serve
500 g/1 lb onions, chopped

2 cloves garlic, chopped
salt and freshly ground
   black pepper
12 Kalamata olives

Warm the oil in a heavy-bottomed frying pan and add the onions and garlic. Stir, cover the pan and cook very gently for 1–1½ hours until the onions have become a golden purée. Season with salt and pepper. Remove from the heat and leave to cool.** Spoon the onion purée on to the pastry, dot with the olives and drizzle on a little olive oil.

Grilled Peppers and Chèvre

2 red peppers, grilled,
   peeled (page 5), seeded,
   then cut into strips
3 small goat's cheeses, each
   about 125 g/4 oz in
   weight

1 tablespoon chopped basil
salt and freshly ground
   black pepper
extra virgin olive oil

Curl the strips of pepper on the pastry to make spirals. Crumble the goat's cheese on top and sprinkle with the basil. Season with salt and pepper and drizzle with olive oil.

** *Can be prepared in advance up to this point.*

Artichokes Stuffed with Crabmeat

The artichokes can be prepared well in advance – even 2–3 days before you intend to use them – provided they are wrapped in cling film and kept refrigerated. Remove the choke just before you stuff them.

SERVES 4

4 large globe artichokes
1 heaped tablespoon flour
900 ml/1 ½ pt water
½ teaspoon salt
juice of 1 lemon

For the stuffing:
2 tablespoons Mayonnaise
   (page 14)

250 g/8 oz white crabmeat
juice of ½ lemon
salt and freshly ground
   black pepper
cayenne pepper
1 tablespoon chopped
   chervil
Vinaigrette with lemon
   (page 16)

Prepare the artichokes one at a time and as you work rub all the cut edges with lemon juice to prevent discoloration.

Cut the stalk off the artichoke and, holding it upside down, bend back the leaves until they snap, then tear them towards the base. Continue until you get to the leaves that curve inwards. With a sharp knife cut these remaining leaves level with the last ring of broken leaf bases. Trim the leaf bases down to the paler flesh. Rub with lemon and put aside while continuing with the rest.

Put the flour into a large pan and gradually whisk in the water. Bring it gently to the boil. Whisk again to make sure that it is smooth and add the salt and lemon juice.

Place the artichokes in the water and simmer for 20–25 minutes until they are tender. Remove them from the pan. When cool, cover and refrigerate until required.**

Mix the mayonnaise into the crabmeat and season with lemon juice, salt and both the peppers. Scoop the choke out of the artichoke with a small spoon. Rinse in cold water, trim off any tough bits and pat dry with kitchen paper. Spoon the crabmeat into the cavity and sprinkle with the chervil. Pour a little lemon vinaigrette on to each plate and put the artichokes in the middle.

** *Can be prepared in advance up to this point.*

Aubergine and Mozzarella Slices with Pepper Sauce

Serve this dish either as a starter or as an accompaniment to grilled meat or fish.

SERVES 4

1 shallot, finely chopped	125 ml/4 fl oz vegetable or
1 clove garlic, chopped	chicken stock
3–4 tablespoons extra	salt and freshly ground
virgin olive oil	black pepper
2 large tomatoes, skinned,	2 large aubergines
seeded and chopped	250 g/8 oz mozzarella,
2 red peppers, grilled, peeled	sliced
(page 5) and seeded	

Sweat the shallot and garlic in 1 tablespoon of oil until soft, then add the tomatoes. Simmer for 5 minutes. Remove from the heat and leave to cool.

Put the peppers into the liquidizer with the tomato mixture and add as much stock as necessary to make a thickish sauce. Season with salt and pepper.**

Heat the grill to maximum temperature.

Cut the aubergines into 1-cm/½-in slices. Brush the slices with the remaining oil and season with salt and pepper. Grill both sides until brown. Cover each slice with a piece of mozzarella and replace under the grill until the cheese is golden.

Serve immediately on top of the warm pepper sauce.

** *Can be prepared in advance up to this point.*

Aubergines Stuffed with Anchovies and Olives

These aubergines make quite a filling starter so follow them with something like a simple fish dish or use them as a light main course served with a green salad.

SERVES 4

2 medium aubergines
salt
125 ml/4 fl oz extra virgin
  olive oil
2 slices of brown bread,
  crusts removed
60 ml/2 fl oz milk
1 tin of anchovy fillets,
  drained and chopped
2 cloves garlic, chopped

16 black olives, stoned and
  chopped
2 tablespoons chopped
  parsley
freshly ground black
  pepper
2–3 tablespoons freshly
  grated Parmesan or
  Pecorino cheese

Cut the stems off the aubergines and slice them in half lengthwise. Score the flesh with a knife, sprinkle with salt and leave to drain for 45 minutes on a rack with the cut sides down. Rinse and wipe dry.

Heat the olive oil in a heavy-bottomed frying pan large enough to take all four aubergine halves at the same time. Cook gently for 20–25 minutes, cut side downwards, until the flesh is soft. Remove them from the pan and allow to cool slightly.

Heat the oven to 190°C/375°F/Gas Mark 5.

Leave the bread to soak in the milk for 5 minutes, then squeeze out the milk and crumble the bread roughly. Scoop the flesh out of the aubergines without damaging the skin and mash it with a fork. Mix in the anchovies, garlic, olives, bread, parsley and pepper. Oil an ovenproof dish and spoon the stuffing into the aubergine skins. Sprinkle with the cheese.** Bake for 20 minutes until the top is golden brown.

** *Can be prepared in advance up to this point.*

Curried Avocado with Bacon

There are two ways of serving this simple yet delicious dish – either in the avocado shells or, if preparation in advance is more convenient, in a bowl topped with the consommé to prevent oxidization.

SERVES 4

1 tin of jellied consommé, if preparing in advance
2 ripe avocados
juice of ½ lemon
½ teaspoon curry powder
2 tablespoons Mayonnaise (page 14)
1 teaspoon Worcestershire sauce

salt and freshly ground black pepper
6–8 rashers of streaky bacon, cooked until crisp then cooled and crumbled

If you are using it, melt the consommé then chill until it starts to thicken but remains pourable.

Halve and scoop out the flesh from the avocados (retaining the shells if necessary) and mash with a fork until smooth. Mix in the lemon juice, curry powder, mayonnaise and Worcestershire sauce. Season with salt and pepper.

Fold in the crumbled bacon and either replace the mixture in the shells or pour it into a shallow bowl. Spoon the consommé very carefully over the avocado so that it stays on the top.** Chill for at least 2 hours before serving.

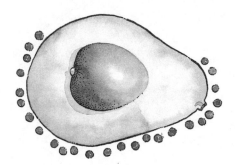

** *Can be prepared in advance up to this point.*

Avocado with Mock Caviar

This is a very quick dish to prepare — leave it to the last minute so that the black juice from the caviar will not discolour the avocado.

SERVES 4

2 ripe avocados
juice of ½ lemon
60 ml/2 fl oz double cream
freshly ground black
   pepper

1 pot of black lumpfish
   roe
salt
2 thin lemon slices, cut in
   half, to serve

Halve the avocados and scoop out the insides, retaining the shells. Mash the flesh with a fork until smooth, then add the lemon juice, double cream and pepper.

Fold in the mock caviar and taste the mixture; add salt only if necessary — it will depend on the saltiness of the caviar.

Replace the avocado mixture in the shells and put the lemon slices on the top.

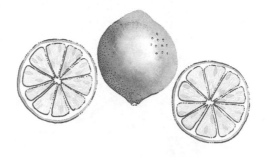

Mushrooms with Sun-dried Tomatoes

This makes good use of the excellent varieties of cultivated mushrooms you can find today. They are gourmet fare with a minimum of fuss. Served cold with Bruschetta (page 46), this recipe makes a tasty starter or can be used hot as a vegetable with grilled fish or meat.

SERVES 4

500 g/1 lb mixed mushrooms, such as field, oyster, or shiitake

2 tablespoons tomato concentrate

125 ml/4 fl oz water

3 tablespoons extra virgin olive oil

1 large onion, finely chopped

2 cloves garlic, finely chopped

150 g/5 oz sun-dried tomatoes, drained and chopped

salt and freshly ground black pepper

Thickly slice the mushrooms or quarter them if they are small. Mix the tomato concentrate, water and olive oil in a large pan, add the onion and garlic, and simmer for 20 minutes. Stir in the mushrooms and sun-dried tomatoes. Simmer for a further 10 minutes. Season with pepper and salt if necessary – this will depend on the saltiness of the tomatoes.**

Serve hot or cold with bruschetta.

** Can be prepared in advance up to this point.

Onion Tartlets with Sun-dried
Tomatoes and Feta Cheese

These little tarts are filled with a delicious mixture of onion confit topped with sun-dried tomatoes and Feta cheese. They make superb starters and can be completely prepared ahead of time. Onion confit, on its own, is very good served with cold game or duck.

SERVES 6

For the confit:	*For the tarts:*
1 kg/2 lb onions	200 g/7 oz Shortcrust
3 tablespoons extra virgin	Pastry (page 19)
olive oil	6–7 sun-dried tomatoes, cut
1 knob of butter	into strips
3 tablespoons sherry	100 g/3½ oz Feta cheese,
vinegar	crumbled
300 ml/½ pt red wine	175 g/6 oz mixed salad
2 teaspoons salt	leaves, lightly dressed
	with a vinaigrette

Slice the onions and place in a large frying pan with the rest of the confit ingredients. Cover the pan and simmer over very low heat for 30 minutes. Remove the lid and simmer another 20 minutes, stirring occasionally with a wooden spoon, until all the moisture has evaporated and the onions are almost a purée.

Make the pastry. Refrigerate for 20 minutes before rolling it out as thinly as possible. Line 6 x 12 cm/4½ in tartlet tins that have removable bases with the pastry. Bake the pastry blind (page 19), reducing the oven time approximately 5 minutes. When cool, remove the pastry from the tins, and store in an airtight container if you are not using it the same day.**

Before serving, pop the pastry back in a moderate oven for a few minutes to crisp up. Warm the confit on top of the cooker. Meanwhile, arrange some salad leaves around six plates. Set the tartlets in the middle, cover with a layer of confit, sprinkle some Feta over the top and decorate with strips of sun-dried tomatoes.

** *Can be prepared in advance up to this point.*

Grilled Mixed Peppers with Polenta

A summer dish redolent of Mediterranean sun. The quality of the olive oil is important in this dish, so try to find an estate-bottled olive oil that is both light and fragrant. Thin wide shavings of Parmesan cheese look attractive and are very good with any number of dishes that call for Parmesan. You need to use a cheese slicer and work with a big piece of fresh Parmesan.

SERVES 4

Polenta (page 22), made
   with 175 g/6 oz polenta
   flour and 900 ml/1 ½ pt
   water
2 red peppers
2 yellow or orange peppers
   or 1 of each
extra virgin olive oil

salt and freshly ground
   black pepper
50 g/2 oz fresh Parmesan
   shavings
12 black olives, stoned and
   chopped
1 tablespoon chopped
   parsley

Cook the polenta and spread it out to form a 2-cm/¾-in layer. Leave until cold, then cut it into eight triangles.**

Cut the peppers into 2.5-cm/1-in strips, discard the seeds and brush with olive oil. Season with salt and pepper. Heat the grill or ridged cast-iron grill pan to maximum temperature and grill the peppers on both sides until they are soft and browned. Remove and keep warm.

Brush the polenta triangles with olive oil and grill them until golden. Arrange them on individual plates with the peppers in untidy layers on top. Scatter with the Parmesan shavings, olives and parsley. Drizzle olive oil over each plate and serve warm.

** *Can be prepared in advance up to this point.*

Roast Shallots and Garlic with Tomatoes on Polenta

Shallots become deliciously sweet when roasted – particularly good are the lozenge-shaped, bronze-skinned variety.

SERVES 4

8 slices of Polenta (page 22), using 100 g/3½ oz polenta flour and 600 ml/ 1 pt water

500 g/1 1b shallots, peeled and cut lengthwise into 4 sections but intact at the base

4 large tomatoes, skinned, seeded and quartered

8 whole cloves garlic, peeled

2 tablespoons extra virgin olive oil

salt and freshly ground black pepper

50 g/2 oz sun-dried tomatoes, chopped

1 tablespoon chopped parsley, to serve

Make the polenta and spread it out to form a 2 cm/¾ in layer. Leave until cold, then cut into slices.**

Heat the oven to 180°C/350°F/Gas Mark 4.

Oil an ovenproof dish and brush the shallots, tomatoes and garlic with olive oil. Season with salt and pepper, cover with foil and bake for 1 hour. Remove from the oven and turn the heat up to 200°C/ 400°F/Gas Mark 6. Lift the tomatoes out of the dish and put into a small saucepan. Mash with a fork, add the sun-dried tomatoes and keep warm. Return the shallots and garlic, uncovered, to the oven and brown them – alternatively, put the dish under a hot grill.

While the shallots are browning, heat a heavy-bottomed frying pan or ridged cast-iron grill pan. Brush the polenta slices with olive oil and cook until golden on both sides.

Place the polenta slices on to warmed plates with the shallots and garlic cloves, then spoon the tomatoes over the top. Sprinkle with parsley and serve.

** *Can be prepared in advance up to this point.*

Baked Summer Vegetables

The range of vegetables you can adapt for this dish is vast, but it is essential to use seasonal and very fresh ones. It is such a simple concept and yet incredibly good. In the heat of the oven while the vegetables soften their natural sugars caramelize, heightening their flavours. This dish can be served as a first course or a light main meal accompanied by grilled or good crusty bread.

SERVES 6

1 kg/2 1b courgettes	12 shallots
3 red onions	2–3 firm aubergines
2 red peppers	salt
2 yellow peppers	extra virgin olive oil
16 small waxy potatoes	grilled bread or warm
6 tomatoes	crusty bread, to serve

Heat the oven to 220°C/425°F/Gas Mark 7.

Wash and dry the vegetables, leaving the skins on all but the onions and shallots. Cut them into large chunks: the courgettes, onions and peppers into four pieces, the potatoes and tomatoes and shallots in half, and the aubergines into four or six pieces.

Divide the vegetables between two baking trays, spreading then out in one layer. Sprinkle them quite lavishly with salt and then pour over a good bit of olive oil. Toss the vegetables with your hands so that they become well impregnated with the oil and salt and spread them out over the trays again.

Bake for about 50 minutes. You will know when they are done when the potatoes are cooked through and the other vegetables are soft and beginning to brown. You can give them a few minutes under the grill if you like them more charred. Arrange a sampling of all the vegetables on individual plates. Serve them warm or at room temperature with the bread.

Baked Winter Vegetables

Replace the summer vegetables with a combination of the following winter vegetables: parsnip, turnip, swede, carrot, celeriac, butternut squash and whole heads of garlic.

Grilled Vegetables

A selection of grilled vegetables can be served on its own with Olive Oil Bread (page 20) to soak up the juices, or the vegetables can be used to accompany grilled fish or meat. You can also dress them up with any number of flavoured oils.

Grilling is a useful and most delicious method of preparing vegetables and brings out their flavours in a stunning way. It can be done over a charcoal grill, under an ordinary grill or in a ridged cast-iron grill pan. If you are making the dish for a large number it speeds things up to use both a pan and another grill source. The vegetables are served at room temperature, so they can be prepared many hours ahead.

SERVES 8

4 courgettes
2 large red or mild Spanish
  onions
3 yellow peppers
6 tomatoes
2 firm aubergines
175 ml/6 fl oz extra virgin
  olive oil

salt and freshly ground or
  crushed black pepper
4 tablespoons chopped
  parsley
4 tablespoons capers
4 tablespoons lemon juice

Preheat the grill. Cut the courgettes and onions into 1 cm/½ in slices. Spear the onion slices with toothpicks to keep them intact. Quarter, core and seed the peppers. Quarter the tomatoes. Just before grilling, cut the aubergine into 1 cm/½ in slices. Discard the end slices, which are mostly skin. Brush the vegetables with olive oil and season with salt and pepper. Start with the aubergines and leave the tomatoes to last. Grill the vegetables on one side until golden brown. Turn them over and repeat on the other side. You want the vegetables to soften without burning, so adjust the heat source accordingly. When the vegetables are done, place them in a large shallow bowl, pour the remaining olive oil over them and sprinkle with the parsley, capers and lemon juice.**

** *Can be prepared in advance.*

LIGHT MAIN COURSES

Butter Bean Soup with Bacon and Leeks

This thick and filling soup makes an excellent winter lunch. Serve it with a green salad and some good bread.

SERVES 4

250 g/8 oz dried butter beans, soaked overnight
50 g/2 oz butter
1 medium onion, finely sliced
1 clove garlic, crushed
2 medium leeks, finely sliced

125 g/4 oz streaky bacon, sliced into 5 mm/¼ in strips
milk, to thin
salt and freshly ground black pepper
1 tablespoon chopped parsley, to serve

Bring the beans to the boil in a large saucepan of fresh water, drain and cover generously with cold water. Simmer until the beans begin to disintegrate. Remove from the heat but do not drain.

Melt the butter in a large saucepan and sauté the onion, garlic, leeks and bacon together until they are soft but not coloured. Add the beans and 300 ml/½ pt of the bean liquid. Remove from the heat and roughly mash some of the beans. Thin with a little more of the bean water and milk until it is the desired consistency. Season with pepper and a little salt if necessary.**

Reheat and stir in the parsley just before serving.

** *Can be prepared in advance up to this point.*

Chicken Livers with Grapes and Pine Nuts

Duck livers, if you can find them, are also delicious cooked to this recipe. To serve this dish as a starter, simply reduce the quantities by half and allow one slice of polenta per person.

SERVES 4

Polenta (page 22)
400 g/14 oz chicken livers
50 g/2 oz butter
2 tablespoons cognac
125 ml/4 fl oz chicken
   stock
175 g/6 oz seedless or Italia
   grapes, peeled and
   pipped

$\frac{1}{4}$ nutmeg, grated
salt and freshly ground
   black pepper
50 g/2 oz pine nuts
extra virgin olive oil

Make the polenta, cut it into eight 8 cm/3 in squares and set them aside.

Pick over the livers and remove any membranes. Melt the butter in a large heavy-bottomed frying pan and sauté the livers until they are brown on all sides but still pink in the middle. Pour the cognac over the livers and flame it. Lift the livers out of the pan and keep them warm.

Place a teaspoon of the fat from the pan into a smaller pan and set aside. Pour away almost all of the rest of the fat from the pan, add the chicken stock, and reduce it with the juices until it begins to thicken. Add the grapes and heat them through. Season with nutmeg, salt and pepper. Replace the livers in the pan and coat them with the sauce.

Toast the pine nuts in the retained fat until golden. Brush the polenta with olive oil and grill on a very hot ridged cast-iron grill pan or under a grill. Serve the chicken livers on the polenta with the pine nuts scattered on the top.

VARIATION:
Replace the grapes with slices of Cox apples that have been sautéed in butter until golden.

Cod Chowder

Fish chowders are hearty and appetizing and unusual enough, at least in this country, to be much appreciated. Haddock can replace the cod and you can vary the shellfish to whatever looks appetizing on the fish counter. Serve with lots of warm bread.

SERVES 6

25 g/1 oz butter
125 g/4 oz streaky bacon, diced
1 medium onion, chopped
1 tablespoon plain flour
450 ml/¾ pt Fish Stock (page 8)
450 ml/¾ pt milk
bouquet garni
4 medium potatoes, diced
1 pinch of mace
salt and freshly ground black pepper
1 pinch of cayenne pepper

750 g/1½ lb cod fillet, skinned and cut into 2.5-cm/1-in cubes
125 g/4 oz small scallops or queens
125 g/4 oz mussels
125 g/4 oz peeled prawns
60 ml/2 fl oz single cream

To serve:
1 tablespoon chopped chives
1 tablespoon chopped parsley

Melt the butter in a large saucepan and brown the bacon and onion. Stir in the flour, cook together for 1 minute, then gradually add the fish stock, followed by the milk. Add the bouquet garni and potatoes. Season with a little mace, salt and both peppers. Simmer until the potatoes are almost cooked,** (if prepared in advance bring back to a simmer when completing) then put in the cod. Bring back to the boil and simmer for 2 minutes. Remove the pan from the heat and stir in the shellfish and cream. Reheat gently but do not allow to boil. Sprinkle with the chives and parsley. Serve immediately before the fish overcooks.

** *Can be prepared in advance up to this point.*

Crostini with Leeks, Pine Nuts and Gruyère

A special open-sandwich piled with delicious ingredients and topped with mozzarella melted under the grill. Good for an informal lunch.

SERVES 4

6 medium leeks
50 g/2 oz butter
½–1 teaspoon harissa sauce
2 tablespoons chopped
  parsley
75 g/3 oz pine nuts

75 g/3 oz grated Gruyère
salt and freshly ground
  black pepper
4 slices good crusty white
  bread, cut from a large
  loaf

Wash the leeks thoroughly and cut them into quarters lengthwise, then slice them finely. Melt most of the butter in a heavy-bottomed frying pan and add the leeks. Cook gently for about 10 minutes, until the leeks are soft, then stir in the harissa and parsley. While the leeks are cooking, heat the remaining butter in a small pan and toast the pine nuts until golden. Sprinkle the Gruyère and pine nuts on the leeks and mix well. Season to taste.

At the same time, grill the bread on both sides. Spread the leeks on the bread and serve.

Crostini with Peppers, Aubergine and Mozzarella

SERVES 4

1 firm large shiny
   aubergine
extra virgin olive oil
salt and freshly ground
   black pepper
1 Ciabatta loaf (page 21)
1 clove garlic, peeled
3 red peppers, grilled,
   peeled (page 5), seeded
   and cut into quarters

8 thin slices of Italian
   salami
2 good-flavoured tomatoes,
   peeled and sliced
250 g/8 oz mozzarella
   cheese, sliced

Cut the aubergine into 1-cm/½-in slices. Brush at once with olive oil and place under a grill until the slices are lightly browned and tender. Season with salt and pepper.**

Cut the ciabatta in half lengthwise and then cut each piece in two. Trim away the crusty ends. Brush with olive oil and toast under the grill. Lightly rub with the garlic.

Lay a few pepper pieces on the bread, then a slice of aubergine, 2 slices of salami, followed by slices of tomato topped with mozzarella.

Place on a rack a little distance from the heat source of the grill for a few minutes so that the vegetables can warm up before the mozzarella burns. Serve at once.

** *Can be prepared in advance up to this point.*

Crostini with Peppers, Gruyère and Anchoïade

Basically this is grilled toast spread with a tasty anchovy butter and topped with a large piece of grilled pepper covered in melting Gruyère – simple but delicious.

SERVES 4

50 g/2 oz tin of anchovies, packed in oil
1 clove garlic, peeled
2 teaspoons vinegar
6–7 tablespoons extra virgin olive oil, plus extra
salt and freshly ground black pepper

3 red peppers, grilled, peeled (page 5) and seeded
125 g/4 oz Gruyère cheese
4 slices good crusty white bread, cut from a large loaf
watercress, to serve

Drain the anchovies. Chop roughly and place in a mortar or bowl. Add the garlic and some black pepper. Use a pestle or wooden spoon and crush to a paste. Stir in the vinegar and slowly, by droplets, stir in the olive oil until you have a thick sauce. Taste for seasoning.

Cut the peppers into three pieces lengthwise. Place them in an oiled baking tin and sprinkle lightly with salt and olive oil. Cut the Gruyère into thin slices.** Place a slice of cheese over each piece of pepper and set under the grill until the cheese melts.

At the same time, grill the bread on both sides. Spread a layer of the anchovy paste on the bread, and arrange three pepper pieces in one layer on top. Cut into three and arrange on individual plates surrounded with the watercress.

** *Can be prepared in advance up to this point.*

Scrambled Eggs with Gruyère and White Wine

Gruyère is much appreciated by the French because it melts well and adds a special nutty flavour. For eating rather than cooking there are two superb French cheeses in the same vein – Beaufort and Comté. Keep an eye out for them – if you appreciate Gruyère you will really enjoy them.

SERVES 4

2 cloves garlic, crushed
250 ml/8 fl oz dry white
    wine
10 free-range eggs
150 g/5 oz freshly grated
    Gruyère

freshly grated nutmeg
salt and coarsely crushed
    black pepper
50 g/2 oz butter

Simmer the crushed garlic and wine in a covered pan for half an hour. The wine should have reduced by more than half. If necessary boil, uncovered, for a few more minutes. Strain and leave to cool.**

Whisk together the eggs, wine, cheese, a little freshly grated nutmeg, salt and pepper.

Melt the butter in a heavy-bottomed frying pan and pour in the egg mixture. Stir constantly, over low heat, until the eggs have thickened but are still creamy.

Serve immediately with a mixed green salad and fresh bread.

** *Can be prepared in advance up to this point.*

Scrambled Eggs with Peppers

This recipe also makes a wonderful frittata; just mix the peppers in with the eggs and cook it gently on both sides as for the Frittata of Caramelized Onions (page 72).

SERVES 4

1 medium onion, finely
   chopped
2 tablespoons extra virgin
   olive oil
2 red peppers, grilled,
   peeled (page 5), seeded
   and finely sliced

2 cloves garlic, chopped
2 tomatoes, peeled, seeded
   and chopped
salt and freshly ground
   black pepper
8 free-range eggs
50 g/2 oz butter

Soften the onion in the olive oil and add the peppers, garlic and tomatoes. Cook together until the juices have evaporated. Season with salt and pepper.** Keep the mixture warm if you are using it straight away.

Beat the eggs, season with salt and pepper and add half of the pepper mixture.

Melt the butter in a heavy-bottomed frying pan and cook the eggs gently, stirring continuously, until they begin to set. Remove the pan from the heat while they are still creamy.

Serve with a spoonful of the remaining pepper mixture in the centre.

** *Can be prepared in advance up to this point.*

Fish Salad with Tomato and Peppers

Make this salad 4–6 hours in advance to allow the flavour of the tomatoes and peppers to permeate the fish while it cools.

SERVES 4

750 g/1½ lb mixed white
  fish, such as cod,
  monkfish, haddock
2 cloves garlic, chopped
salt and freshly ground
  black pepper
450 ml/¾ pt Tomato Sauce
  (page 12)

1 red pepper, grilled,
  peeled (page 5), seeded
  and finely sliced
2 shallots, finely chopped
1 tablespoon chopped
  coriander
2 tablespoons extra virgin
  olive oil

Heat the oven to 190°C/375°F/Gas Mark 5.

Skin and cut the fish into 2.5 cm/1 in cubes and place it in an oiled ovenproof dish. Sprinkle on the garlic and season with salt and pepper. Pour the tomato sauce over the fish and lay the pepper strips on top. Cover with foil and cook for 20 minutes.

Remove from the oven and leave to cool.** Before serving, sprinkle on the shallots and coriander, then drizzle on the olive oil.

Serve with Bruschetta (page 46) and a green salad.

** *Can be prepared in advance up to this point.*

Fish in Spicy Yoghurt Sauce

The joy of this dish is that it really is best made the day before and left in the refrigerator overnight. Take it out at least one hour before serving.

SERVES 4

250 g/8 oz red onions, cut into quarters and finely sliced
1 kg/2 lb cod or haddock, skinned and cut crosswise into 4-cm/1½-in thick strips
salt and freshly ground black pepper

1 tablespoon lemon or lime juice
2 teaspoons ground cumin
¼ teaspoon mace
¼ teaspoon cayenne pepper
3 tablespoons extra virgin olive oil
450 ml/¾ pt plain yoghurt
2 tablespoons finely chopped coriander

Heat the oven to 190°C/375°F/Gas Mark 5.

Put the onions into an oiled shallow ovenproof dish and place the fish on top in a single layer. Season with salt and pepper. Mix the lemon or lime juice, cumin, mace, cayenne pepper and 2 tablespoons of olive oil into the yoghurt, and pour over the fish. Cover with foil and bake for 30 minutes.

Remove from the oven and leave to cool for at least 5 hours or overnight.**

Lift out the fish with its covering of yoghurt and arrange it on a serving dish with the onions. Pour enough of the separated juices over the top to moisten them. Sprinkle with the coriander and the remaining olive oil.

Serve with a green salad and Bruschetta (page 46).

** *Can be prepared in advance up to this point.*

Frittata of Mixed Mushrooms

A frittata is a thick omelette which can be filled with any number of different vegetables or meats. It is cooked very slowly so the eggs remain tender. This mushroom frittata is much creamier than most frittatas – really more of a quiche without the crust. It is served in wedges accompanied by extra mushrooms. You can add a salad or some potatoes to complete the meal.

SERVES 4

2 shallots	juice of $\frac{1}{2}$ lemon
1 clove garlic	salt and freshly ground
3 tablespoons extra virgin	black pepper
olive oil	8 free-range eggs
150 g/5 oz oyster	150 ml/$\frac{1}{4}$ pt double or
mushrooms, finely sliced	whipping cream
300 g/10 oz chestnut	15 g/$\frac{1}{2}$ oz butter
mushrooms, finely sliced	

Sauté the shallots and garlic in 2 tablespoons of the oil until they are translucent. Add the mushrooms, lemon juice and some salt and pepper, and stir over a medium heat until the mushrooms begin to give off their juices. Raise the heat to evaporate most of the liquid.

Beat the eggs and cream together and season well. Stir half of the mushrooms into the eggs.

Heat the oven to 150°C/300°F/Gas Mark 2.

Heat the remaining oil and the butter in an ovenproof frying pan, preferably cast iron. Pour in the egg mixture and cook over a very low heat until the bottom is just beginning to set. Place the pan in the oven until the top has barely set – about 15–20 minutes. Reheat the extra mushrooms. Serve wedges of the frittata on individual plates with some mushrooms around the edge.

Frittata of Caramelized Onions and
Sun-dried Tomatoes

Frittatas are extremely versatile. You can vary the fillings and they can be served cold as well as hot – the perfect solution for your next picnic.

SERVES 4

500g/1 lb onions, finely
    sliced
5 tablespoons extra virgin
    olive oil
8 free-range eggs

125 g/4 oz sun-dried
    tomatoes, drained and
    chopped
salt and freshly ground
    black pepper

Cook the onions gently in a heavy-bottomed frying pan with 4 table-spoons of the oil until they have caramelized, about 30 minutes.**

Beat the eggs and mix in the sun-dried tomatoes, followed by the onions. Season with pepper and a little salt depending on the saltiness of the tomatoes.

Using the same pan, heat the final tablespoon of oil and pour in the egg mixture, turn down the heat and cook gently without stirring for about 10 minutes until it has nearly set.

Place the pan under a heated grill to set the top or turn the frittata over by sliding it on to a large plate then back into the pan for a minute. Alternatively, finish off the cooking in an oven preheated to 150°C/300°F/Gas Mark 2. Serve hot or cold.

VARIATION
Omit the sun-dried tomatoes and replace them with a grilled red pepper and 75 g/3 oz grated Fontina cheese.

** *Can be prepared in advance up to this point.*

Frittata of Potato and Sorrel

Potatoes, onion and sorrel (or spinach) may not seem that exciting a combination but they work magic in this frittata. It tastes terrific.

SERVES 4

4–6 well-flavoured potatoes such as Charlotte, Belle de Fontenay or La Ratte – choose the larger potatoes from these small-size varieties
1 tablespoon extra virgin olive oil
50g/2 oz butter
1 medium onion, chopped

8 free-range eggs
1 generous handful of sorrel, washed, stripped off the stalks and chopped, or 250 g/8 oz spinach, wilted then chopped with a little lemon juice added
salt and freshly ground black pepper

Boil the potatoes in their skins until they are just cooked. Drain, skin and cut them into 1 cm/½ in cubes. Heat the olive oil and 25g/1 oz butter in a large frying pan and sauté the onion until it is golden. Add the potatoes and cook together until they are lightly coloured. Stir in the sorrel or spinach and season with salt and pepper.**

Whisk the eggs with a little more salt and pepper. Add the remaining 25 g/1 oz butter to the pan and when it has melted pour in the eggs. Cook gently without stirring for about 10 minutes until the frittata has almost set.

Place the pan under a heated grill to brown the top or turn the frittata over by sliding it on to a large plate then back into the pan for a minute or two. Alternatively, finish off the cooking in an oven preheated to 150°C/300°F/Gas Mark 2. Serve hot or cold with a green salad.

** *Can be prepared in advance up to this point.*

Creamy Moules Marinières

Mussels are easy to deal with at home and they make a very good light meal or first course.

SERVES 4

1.75 kg/4 lb mussels
2 shallots, finely chopped
1 clove garlic, chopped
  (optional)
25 g/1 oz butter
2 tablespoons extra virgin
  olive oil
150 ml/¼ pt dry white wine

bouquet garni
salt and freshly ground
  black pepper
4 tablespoons double cream
4 tablespoons finely
  chopped parsley, to
  serve

Scrub the mussels with a hard brush and drop them into a large pail of cold lightly salted water. They can be left for 12 hours. When you are ready to cook them, discard any that have opened. Pull off the beards with your fingers and rinse under cold running water.

Sweat the shallots and garlic in the butter and olive oil in a large saucepan. When the shallots are soft, pour in the wine and bring to the boil. Add the mussels, the bouquet garni and some salt and pepper. Raise the heat and cook the mussels for 4–5 minutes, shaking the pan once or twice so that the mussels cook evenly.

Scoop out the mussels with a large flat sieve and place in a large heated tureen or individual heated soup bowls. Strain the cooking liquid through a muslin-lined sieve into a wide shallow saucepan or sauté pan. Boil hard to reduce the liquid by half. Add the cream and bring back to the boil. Pour over the mussels and sprinkle with the parsley. Serve at once with good crusty bread.

Pepper and Anchovy Soufflé

Grilled peppers and anchovies give a wonderfully fragrant taste to this soufflé.

SERVES 4

25 g/1 oz butter
1 tablespoon flour
250 ml/8 fl oz milk
2 red peppers, grilled, peeled (page 5) and seeded
10 anchovy fillets, cut into small pieces

salt and freshly ground black pepper
5 free-range egg yolks
grated Parmesan or Pecorino cheese
6 free-range egg whites

Melt the butter and stir in the flour, and cook together over low heat for 1 minute. Slowly pour in the milk, stirring all the time, then bring to the boil and simmer for 2 minutes. The mixture should be quite thick.

Place the peppers in the bowl of a food processor and whiz until smooth. Stir in the chopped anchovy fillets and check the seasonings. Pour the purée into the sauce and mix well. Beat in the egg yolks, one at a time.

Heat the oven to 200°C/400°F/Gas Mark 6. Generously butter a 1.25 L/2¼ pt soufflé dish, sprinkle with the grated Parmesan or Pecorino. Tip the dish to distribute the cheese evenly.

Whisk the egg whites with a pinch of salt until they form soft peaks. Using a large metal spoon, first fold a dollop of the whites into the egg yolk mixture to lighten it, then carefully fold in the rest. Pour the mixture into the centre of the soufflé dish, making sure that there are no drips on the sides to prevent it from rising evenly. Bake for 12–15 minutes and serve immediately.

Pissaladière

The name for this succulent Provençal onion tart comes from 'pissala', a purée of tiny fish preserved in brine which is sometimes still used in place of the more usual anchovies. Pissaladière is a cross between a quiche and a pizza and can be made with either bread dough or puff pastry.

For the dough:
200 g/7 oz plain or strong
    flour
1 teaspoon salt
¾ teaspoon easy blend dried
    yeast
90 ml/3 fl oz water
1 small egg

For the topping:
4 tablespoons extra virgin
    olive oil

1 kg/2 lb mild Spanish
    onions, sliced
1 teaspoon thyme
salt and freshly ground
    black pepper
4 tomatoes, skinned and
    sliced
8 anchovy fillets
6 sun-dried tomatoes, cut
    into slivers (optional)
12 small black olives,
    stoned

To make the dough, place the flour and salt in a bowl and mix in the yeast. Add the water and egg and stir together until the mixture forms a mass. Turn the dough out on to a floured board and knead until soft and smooth, adding a bit more flour if the dough is too sticky. Place in a greased bowl, cover with a damp cloth and leave to rise in a warm place for 1 hour or until doubled in size. Meanwhile, heat the oil in a heavy frying pan, add the onions, thyme and some salt and pepper. Cover and cook over a very low heat for 25 minutes. Remove the lid and continue to cook, stirring occasionally, until the onions are very soft and golden – almost a purée.**

Place a baking sheet in the centre of the oven and preheat to 190°C/375°F/Gas Mark 5.

When the dough has risen, punch it down and roll out on a floured board. Place it in an oiled 30 cm/12 in pie or pizza pan and stretch it out so that the crust is slightly higher on the sides. Spoon the onions on to the crust. Arrange the tomatoes on top and make a lattice pattern with the anchovies and sun-dried tomatoes, if you are using them. Place the olives in the gaps. Leave to rise for at least 30 minutes. Bake on the hot oven sheet for 30 minutes. Serve warm.

** *Can be prepared in advance up to this point.*

Potatoes Normandy

An attractive and delicious potato dish that is almost a complete meal in itself. It is also a very good way of using leftover ham or gammon. Serve with a salad for a light lunch.

SERVES 2–3

1 onion, finely chopped
50 g/2 oz butter, plus extra
4 leeks, finely sliced
250 g/8 oz chopped cooked
   ham or gammon, diced
750 g/1½ lb waxy potatoes,
   sliced very finely
2 tablespoons chopped
   parsley

freshly grated nutmeg
salt and freshly ground
   black pepper
300 ml/½ pt Chicken Stock
   (page 7)
150 ml/¼ pt single cream

Heat the oven to 170°C/325°F/Gas Mark 3.

Soften the onion in the butter, add the leeks and stir together until they have wilted. Remove from the heat and mix in the diced ham.

Butter an ovenproof dish and make alternate layers of the sliced potatoes and the leek mixture. Sprinkle parsley, nutmeg, salt and pepper in between the layers. Finish with an overlapping layer of potatoes.

Bring the stock to the boil in a small pan and pour it over the potatoes – the top layer should not quite be covered. Dot with a little more butter. Bake in the oven for 1 hour, or until the potatoes are cooked.

Spoon the cream over the top and replace in the oven for 5 minutes to heat through.

Prawn and Fish Couscous

The instructions below are for serving the couscous hot but it also makes a very good salad. Simply follow the recipe as far as the asterisks but reduce the stock to 350 ml/12 fl oz. Fluff the couscous up with a fork, season with salt and pepper and add extra olive oil and lemon juice. Combine with all the remaining ingredients when the couscous has cooled.

SERVES 4

250 g/8 oz cod or haddock
  fillet
2 tablespoons extra virgin
  olive oil
2 cloves garlic, chopped
3 shallots, chopped
1 pinch of mace
400 ml/14 fl oz Fish or
  Chicken Stock (pages 7, 8)
250 g/8 oz couscous
salt and freshly ground
  black pepper

250 g/8 oz peeled prawns
1 red pepper, grilled,
  peeled (page 5), seeded
  and sliced
125 g/4 oz petit pois,
  defrosted
2 tablespoons chopped
  parsley
a bunch of chives, finely
  snipped, to serve

Heat the oven to 190°C/375°F/Gas Mark 5 and bake the seasoned fish fillet in an oiled ovenproof dish for 10 minutes. Leave to cool, then flake.

Warm the oil and garlic in a large saucepan and add the shallots. Cook gently until they are soft but not coloured. Sprinkle with the mace, heat together for 1 minute, then pour in the stock. Bring to the boil, add the couscous, stir and remove from the heat. Cover and leave for 10 minutes until the stock has been absorbed.** Season with salt and pepper and using a heat diffuser, gently reheat with the fish, prawns, pepper, peas and parsley.

Sprinkle on the chives before serving.

** *Can be prepared in advance up to this point.*

Salad Niçoise with fresh tuna

Any number of different ingredients can be used for this classic salad, such as artichoke hearts, thin slivers of raw fennel, broad beans or indeed any of the baby vegetables now available.

SERVES 6

For the tuna:
750 g/1½ lb fresh tuna steaks, 2 cm/¾ in thick
3 tablespoons extra virgin olive oil
several leaves of fresh basil, shredded, plus extra to serve
1 tablespoon lemon juice
salt and freshly ground black pepper

For the vinaigrette:
125 ml/4 fl oz extra virgin olive oil
4 tablespoons wine vinegar
1 squeeze of lemon juice
salt and freshly ground black pepper

For the salad:
250 g/8 oz fresh small green beans
leaves from 3 different lettuces
4 eggs, hard boiled, shelled and quartered
8 new potatoes, boiled and sliced
6 firm ripe tomatoes, skinned and cut into wedges
8 anchovy fillets
1 small handful of little black olives
½ cucumber, peeled and sliced
4 spring onions, finely sliced

Marinate the tuna in the olive oil, basil and lemon juice for a few hours if possible. Season with salt and pepper. Heat the grill or ridged cast-iron grill pan until very hot, then grill the fish for about 3 minutes on each side. Remove the fish to a plate to cool.

Meanwhile, blanch the beans in a large amount of boiling salted water until barely tender. Refresh under cold running water and drain.**

Make the vinaigrette and use half to dress the lettuce. Arrange some leaves on six plates. Make individual piles of the other ingredients and arrange pieces of the tuna around the edge. Spoon some dressing over the beans and other ingredients but leave the tuna plain. Alternatively, you can mix the ingredients in a more casual way and set the tuna on top. Sprinkle some basil on the salad before serving.

** *Can be prepared in advance up to this point.*

Spinach Torta

Another very useful all-in-one dish that is also good for vegetarians if you change the chicken stock to a vegetable one.

SERVES 4–6

750 g/1 ½ lb fresh spinach
3 tablespoons extra virgin olive oil
150 g/5 oz tomatoes, peeled, seeded and chopped
1 clove garlic, finely chopped
135 g/4 ½ oz arborio rice
350 ml/12 fl oz Chicken Stock (page 7)

4 free-range eggs
40 g/1 ½ oz freshly grated Parmesan cheese
a few gratings of fresh nutmeg
salt and freshly ground black pepper
50 g/2 oz dry breadcrumbs

Wash the spinach carefully and chop coarsely. Heat the oil in a large saucepan and sauté the tomatoes for a few minutes, then add the garlic and cook for a further few minutes. Add the spinach and some salt and stir from time to time until the spinach wilts. Add the rice and a ladleful of the stock. Stir from time to time, uncovered, adding more stock as necessary until the rice is partially cooked – about 15 minutes.**

Heat the oven to 190°C/375°F/Gas Mark 5.

Oil a round or rectangular ovenproof dish approximately 20 cm/8 in in diameter (900 ml/1 ½ pt capacity). Beat the eggs and add them to the spinach along with the grated cheese and nutmeg. Season with salt and pepper. Pour into the oven dish, sprinkle with the breadcrumbs and bake for 50 minutes. Serve lukewarm in slices.

** *Can be prepared in advance up to this point.*

Stuffed Squid with Tomato Concassé

Harissa sauces vary in their chilli-heat so add it a little at a time to the stuffing mixture – in the finished dish it is balanced by the cooling tomato concassé.

SERVES 4

10 anchovy fillets, mashed
100 g/3½ oz fresh
    breadcrumbs
1–2 teaspoons harissa sauce
2 tablespoons chopped
    coriander
12 squid, 10 cm/4 in long,
    cleaned (page 6),
    tentacles retained

2–3 tablespoons extra
    virgin olive oil
salt and freshly ground
    black pepper
250 g/8 oz Tomato Concassé
    (page 6)

To make the stuffing, mix the anchovies into the breadcrumbs and add harissa sauce to taste. Mash together until smooth and stir in the coriander and the chopped tentacles. Moisten with enough olive oil to make a firm paste. Season with salt and pepper. Stuff the body cavities of the squid with the mixture, using your fingers or a small spoon, and place in an oiled ovenproof dish. Brush with olive oil and season.**

Heat the oven to 200°C/400°F/Gas Mark 6.

Bake for 7 minutes, then pour in the tomato concassé and drizzle with olive oil. Replace in the oven for a further 4–5 minutes. Serve immediately.

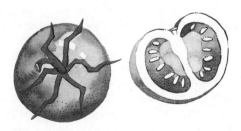

** *Can be prepared in advance up to this point.*

Spicy Tortilla

The Spanish tortilla is a close relation to the Italian frittata and every bit as tasty. Delicious eaten warm or cold. Serve with a green salad.

SERVES 4

300 g/10 oz waxy potatoes such as Belle de Fontenay, Charlotte, Nicola or La Ratte
1–2 heaped teaspoons harissa sauce
salt and freshly ground black pepper
50 g/2 oz sun-dried tomatoes, drained and finely sliced

2 tablespoons chopped coriander
25 g/1 oz butter
4 tablespoon extra virgin olive oil
1 clove garlic, chopped
3 shallots, finely chopped
1 small red pepper, shredded very finely
3 eggs

Gently boil the potatoes in their skins until they are just cooked; do not allow them to disintegrate. When they are cool, skin them, dice finely and toss with the harissa sauce. Season with salt and pepper and stir in the sun-dried tomatoes and coriander.**

Heat the butter and 2 tablespoons of oil in a heavy-bottomed frying pan and cook the garlic, shallots and pepper gently until they are soft. Mix with the potato. Check the seasoning and add a little more harissa sauce if necessary. Beat the eggs, season with salt and pepper and fold into the vegetables.

For the oven method: Heat the oven to 130°C/250°F/Gas Mark ½ and warm the remaining oil in an ovenproof heavy-bottomed frying pan approximately 20 cm/8 in in diameter. Pour in the mixture which should be about 2 cm/1 in thick and place in the oven for 20–25 minutes until set.

For the hob method: Cook the tortilla on as low a heat as possible – a heat diffuser is useful here. Cook without stirring for 25–30 minutes until all but the very top layer is set. Slide the tortilla on to a plate and invert it back into the pan or place under a hot grill for a few minutes to set the top. Tip the tortilla on to a serving plate and allow to cool slightly. Cut into slices like a cake.

** *Can be prepared in advance up to this point.*

PASTA

What would we do without pasta? It serves the most unambitious cook as well as the starred chef and everyone in between. Fresh egg pasta is widely available and perfectly adequate but it doesn't compare to egg pasta made at home. This is particularly true for lasagnes and stuffed pastas, where the lightness of the pasta and the scope of stuffings are unrivalled by any commercial product. The instructions below are for making pasta using a hand-cranking machine. Each time you make it you will find it easier and faster to do.

Basic Egg Pasta

MAKES ABOUT 500 g/1 lb PASTA

125 g/4 oz semolina
185 g/6½ oz plain
  unbleached flour

½ teaspoon salt
3 eggs, lightly beaten

METHOD 1
Put the semolina and plain flour on a work surface, make a well in the middle, sprinkle on the salt and add the eggs. Gradually mix in the flour from the sides and knead until a dough is formed. Cover and leave to rest for at least 30 minutes.

METHOD 2
Put all the ingredients into the bowl of a food processor and process until the dough forms a ball. Cover and leave to rest for at least 30 minutes.

Take a lump of the dough the size of a lemon. The dough should not be too moist or it will stick to the machine. Dust with flour if necessary. Feed it through the rollers set on the widest opening. Crank the piece through. Fold it in half, end to end, and feed it through again six or seven times until the dough is a smooth and elastic rectangle. Lay out on a clean cloth or floured surface and repeat with the remaining dough. Reset the rollers to the next setting down and, starting with the first strip, crank it through the rollers, but only once. Repeat with the other strips, keeping the order the same to allow the dough to dry slightly. Repeat, resetting the roller each time, until the strips are all the desired thinness. (Cut the strips in half when they become too long to handle.) Feed the strips through the tagliatelle cutters and leave to dry slightly, either separated on a surface sprinkled with semolina or hanging over a clean broom handle. If the pasta is to be used for lasagne or a stuffed recipe, use the pasta lengths without cutting or drying them.

Garlic Pasta

Add 2 cloves crushed garlic to the eggs.

Herb Pasta

Add 2 tablespoons very finely chopped herbs (parsley, basil, chervil, coriander) to the eggs.

Saffron Pasta

Add $\frac{1}{2}$ teaspoon of saffron powder to the eggs.

Spinach Pasta

Add 50 g/2 oz of blanched and very well-drained spinach purée to the eggs.

Sun-dried Tomato Pasta

Add 2 tablespoons sun-dried tomato purée to the eggs.

Buckwheat Pasta

This goes particularly well with Fresh and Sun-dried Tomato Sauce (page 87) and Grilled Vegetables (page 60).

125 g/4 oz buckwheat flour	65 g/2½ oz semolina
125 g/4 oz plain unbleached flour	3 eggs, lightly beaten
	½ teaspoon salt

Follow the recipe for Basic Egg Pasta (page 83), using the above ingredients. Buckwheat pasta takes a little longer to cook – about 2–3 minutes.

Thirteen Pasta Dishes

All of the following pasta recipes can be made with fresh, bought or home-made egg pasta. Any of the flat shapes such as tagliatelle, fettucine or the thinner linguine can be used.

Pasta with Broccoli Florets and Nasturtium Butter

Paper-thin slices of Parmesan are made by drawing a cheese slicer across a large piece of fresh cheese. The golden slices look attractive and make a change from the more usual grated cheese. It is often used over warm asparagus that has been dressed with extra virgin olive oil.

SERVES 4–6

1 head of broccoli, stalk
   removed and head
   broken into tiny florets
500 g/1 1b fresh pasta
Nasturtium Butter
   (page 13), made with
   125 g/4 oz butter

salt and freshly ground
   black pepper
50 g/2 oz fresh Parmesan
   shavings

Cook the broccoli in salted water for 1–2 minutes then drain. At the same time, cook the pasta in a large quantity of boiling salted water and drain. Toss the cooked pasta in the nasturtium butter, mix in the broccoli and season with salt and pepper. Serve topped with the Parmesan shavings.

Pasta with Duck or Chicken Livers and Green Beans

SERVES 4–6

50 g/2 oz pine nuts
4–5 tablespoons extra
  virgin olive oil
175 g/6 oz green beans, cut
  into 2.5-cm/1-in pieces
250 g/8 oz duck or chicken
  livers
1 tablespoon balsamic
  vinegar

salt and freshly ground
  black pepper
4 shallots, finely sliced
500 g/1 lb fresh pasta
2 tablespoons chopped
  parsley

Lightly brown the pine nuts in 1 teaspoon of olive oil. Drain on kitchen paper.

Cook the beans in boiling salted water and drain.

Pick over the livers and remove any fatty pieces. Heat 2 tablespoons of olive oil in a heavy-bottomed frying pan and sauté the livers over a high heat until they are browned but still pink on the inside. Pour in the balsamic vinegar and season with salt and pepper. Stir together, then remove the livers from the pan, slice them and keep warm. Add a little more oil to the pan and soften the shallots. Add the beans to the pan and heat through.

At the same time, cook the pasta in a large pan of salted water. Drain and toss with 2 tablespoons of olive oil. Mix with the chicken livers, pine nuts, shallots, beans and parsley. Season and serve.

Pasta with Fresh and Sun-dried Tomatoes

Buckwheat pasta is slightly grainy which helps the sauce to adhere to the pasta. It is particularly successful with a simple sauce such as this tomato one.

SERVES 4–6

2 cloves garlic, crushed
2 tablespoons extra virgin
   olive oil, plus extra
750 g/1 ½ lb ripe tomatoes,
   skinned, seeded and
   finely chopped
175 g/6 oz sun-dried
   tomatoes, drained and
   sliced

salt and freshly ground
   black pepper
1 generous handful of basil
   leaves, chopped
500 g/1 lb fresh pasta

Place a large pan of salted water on the hob and bring to the boil.

Heat the garlic in the olive oil, add the tomatoes and reduce to a medium thickness. Stir in the sun-dried tomatoes, season with salt and pepper and heat through. Remove from the heat ** and add the basil.

Plunge the pasta into the boiling water and cook for 2–3 minutes. Drain and toss in a little extra virgin olive oil. Pour the hot sauce over the pasta and serve.

** *Can be prepared in advance up to this point.*

Pasta with Garlic, Parsley and Anchovies

SERVES 4–6

500 g/1 lb fresh pasta
125 ml/4 fl oz extra virgin
  olive oil
4–6 cloves garlic, finely
  chopped

1 tin of anchovy fillets,
  drained and chopped
grated rind of 1 lemon
2 tablespoons chopped
  parsley
salt and freshly ground
  black pepper

While the pasta is cooking, heat the oil in a pan and gently sauté the garlic but do not allow it to brown. Add the chopped anchovies, lemon and parsley, and season with salt and pepper. Pour the mixture over the drained pasta.

Pasta with Garlic Sauce

The amount of garlic in this recipe may seem excessive but when it is braised its flavour mellows. The garlic is then simmered in a little cream – it makes a most fragrant and simple pasta sauce.

SERVES 4–6

2 large heads of fresh garlic
50 g/2 oz butter
300 ml/½ pt whipping cream
8 sun-dried tomatoes, sliced

500 g/1 lb fresh pasta
salt and freshly ground
  black pepper

Separate the cloves of garlic and place in a small pan of simmering water. Leave for 30 seconds, then drain. Place the cloves on a chopping board, cut a sliver off the base end and slip off the skins.

Place the peeled cloves and butter in a heavy-based small saucepan and simmer over very low heat for 10–15 minutes, until very tender. The cloves should not colour more than a creamy yellow. Add the cream, some salt and pepper, and simmer over low heat for 5–10 minutes. Remove from the heat and crush the garlic with a potato masher or fork, until you have a creamy purée.** Keep the sauce warm.

Bring a large quantity of water to the boil, add 2 tablespoons of salt and when the water returns to the boil throw in the pasta. Cook until *al dente* – with a bit of bite left in it. Drain, but do not overdrain or shake the colander. Turn into a heated bowl. Pour over the garlic sauce and sun-dried tomatoes. Toss together and serve.

** *Can be prepared in advance up to this point.*

Pasta with Grilled Summer Vegetables

This recipe also makes a delicious topping for a pizza. Spread the tomato sauce over the pizza, cover with the grilled vegetables and bake.

SERVES 4–6

1 red, yellow and green
   pepper, each grilled,
   peeled (page 5) and
   seeded
2 small aubergines, finely
   sliced
extra virgin olive oil
4 shallots, cut into fine
   rings

500 g/1 lb fresh pasta
350 ml/12 fl oz Tomato
   Sauce (page 12)
salt and freshly ground
   black pepper
2 tablespoons chopped
   parsley, to serve

Slice the peppers into 1 cm/½ in strips.

Heat a ridged cast-iron grill pan to maximum temperature. Brush the aubergines with olive oil, grill on both sides and cut into 1 cm/½ in strips. Brush the shallot rings with olive oil and grill until soft and brown.

Cook the pasta in a large quantity of boiling salted water, then drain. At the same time, warm the tomato sauce and mix in all the grilled vegetables. Pour over the pasta, check the seasoning, and sprinkle with the parsley.

Pasta with Prawns, Peas and Mint

SERVES 4–6

500 g/1 lb fresh pasta
2 cloves garlic, chopped
2 tablespoons extra virgin
   olive oil
175 g/6 oz peas, fresh or
   defrosted
salt and freshly ground
   black pepper

350 g/12 oz shelled prawns
1 handful of fresh mint
   leaves, chopped
175 ml/6 fl oz crème
   fraîche

Cook the pasta in a large quantity of boiling salted water and drain.

At the same time, in a saucepan, warm the garlic in the oil and add the peas. Season with salt and pepper and heat for 1 minute. Add the prawns, mint and crème fraîche and heat through. Pour over the hot drained pasta.

Pasta with Salmon, Green Beans and Tapenade

SERVES 4–6

250 g/8 oz salmon fillet
500 g/1 lb fresh pasta
250 g/8 oz fine green beans,
   cut into 2.5 cm/1 in
   pieces

4 tablespoons Tapenade
   (page 11)
extra virgin olive oil
salt and freshly ground
   black pepper

Heat the oven to 190°C/375°F/Gas Mark 5 and bake the salmon in an oiled ovenproof dish for 10 minutes. Cool and flake.

Cook the pasta in a large quantity of boiling salted water, then drain. At the same time, cook the beans for 2 minutes in another saucepan of boiling salted water. Drain the beans and add to the pasta with the salmon. Toss with the tapenade and a little more olive oil if it seems too dry. Check seasoning and serve.

Pasta with Smoked Salmon Butter and Chives

SERVES 4–6

500 g/1 lb fresh pasta
Smoked Salmon Butter
   (page 13) made with
   175 g/6 oz butter and
   175 g/6 oz smoked
   salmon pieces

salt and coarsely crushed
   black pepper
4–5 tablespoons chives,
   finely snipped, to serve

Cook the pasta in a large quantity of boiling salted water. Drain the pasta and toss with the butter. Season with pepper and a little salt if necessary. Sprinkle with chives and serve.

Pasta with Squid and Tomato Sauce

SERVES 4–6

1 clove garlic, crushed
4–6 tablespoons extra
   virgin olive oil
1 kg/2 lb ripe tomatoes,
   skinned, seeded and
   finely chopped

500 g/1 lb small squid,
   cleaned (page 6) and cut
   into rings with the
   tentacles retained
salt and freshly ground
   black pepper
2 tablespoons chopped
   basil
500 g/1 lb fresh pasta

Heat the garlic in the olive oil, add the tomatoes and reduce the sauce to a medium thickness. Add the squid rings and tentacles, and simmer for 2–3 minutes, until tender. Season with salt and pepper. Remove from the heat ** and stir in the basil.

Bring a large pan of salted water to the boil and plunge the pasta in for about 1 minute. Drain and toss in a little olive oil. Pour the hot sauce over the pasta and serve immediately.

** *Can be prepared in advance up to this point.*

Pasta with Squid, White Wine and Cream

SERVES 4–6

50 g/2 oz butter
2 cloves garlic, finely
   chopped
500 g/1 lb small squid,
   cleaned (page 6), sacs
   cut into fine rings, and
   tentacles cut into pieces
90 ml/3 fl oz white wine

salt and freshly ground
   black pepper
500 g/1 lb fresh pasta
extra virgin olive oil
150 ml/¼ pt single cream
2 tablespoons chopped
   parsley

Place a large pan of salted water on the hob and bring to the boil.

Heat the butter in a large heavy-bottomed frying pan and warm the garlic. Raise the heat to moderate, add the squid and stir together for 2 minutes. Pour in the wine, season with salt and pepper, and simmer until the squid is just cooked. This should only take 2–3 minutes depending on the size of the squid – take care, overcooking squid makes them rubbery.

Plunge the pasta into the boiling water for 1 minute. Drain and toss it in a little olive oil.

Pour the cream into the squid and heat through but do not allow it to boil. Check the seasoning, stir in the parsley and pour over the pasta. Serve immediately.

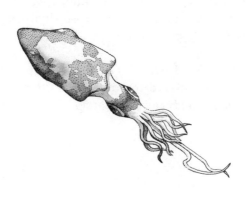

Pasta with Tuna, Olives and Parsley

SERVES 4

250 g/8 oz fresh tuna steak,
  1 cm/½ in thick
125 ml/4 fl oz extra virgin
  olive oil
salt and freshly ground
  black pepper
peeled rind of 1 lemon,
  finely chopped

2 cloves garlic, chopped
20 Kalamata olives, stoned
2 tablespoons capers
500 g/1 lb fresh pasta
2 tablespoons chopped
  parsley

Brush the tuna with olive oil and season with salt and pepper. Using a heavy-bottomed frying pan, sauté each side for 1 minute. Cool and flake the tuna into a small saucepan. Add 60 ml/2 fl oz of the olive oil, lemon rind, garlic, olives and capers, and warm through over a gentle heat. At the same time, cook the pasta in a large quantity of boiling salted water. Drain and toss with the remaining olive oil and the parsley. Add the tuna mixture and serve.

Pasta with Wild Mushrooms and Chicken

SERVES 4–6

15 g/½ oz dried porcini
  mushrooms
250 ml/8 fl oz mushroom
  water (see below)
2 tablespoons extra virgin
  olive oil
2 cloves garlic, chopped
4 shallots, chopped
2 free-range chicken
  breasts, skinned and
  finely sliced crosswise
  into 5 mm/¼ in strips

1 teaspoon fresh thyme,
  chopped
salt and freshly ground
  black pepper
500 g/1 lb fresh pasta

To serve:
1 teaspoon extra virgin
  olive oil
50 g/2 oz pine nuts
2 tablespoons chopped
  parsley

Soak the mushrooms in water for 30 minutes and rub off any grit. Drain, filter the soaking liquid and finely slice the mushrooms. Reduce the mushroom water over a high heat to about 125 ml/ 4 fl oz.**

Heat the olive oil and sauté the garlic and shallots until they are golden, then add the chicken. Stir together for a few minutes to seal the chicken and toss in the mushrooms and thyme. Pour in the mushroom liquid and simmer together until the chicken and mushrooms are tender – about 5 minutes. Season with salt and pepper.

While the chicken is cooking, warm the olive oil in a small frying pan and sauté the pine nuts until they are golden.

Cook the pasta in a large quantity of boiling salted water, and drain. Pour the sauce over the pasta, sprinkle with the pine nuts and parsley, and serve.

** *Can be prepared in advance up to this point.*

Lasagne with Chicken and Mushrooms

Any meat left over from a roast chicken can be used instead of the chicken breasts; simply add the chopped pieces to the onions at the same time as the mushrooms and tarragon.

SERVES 6

500 g/1 lb Basic Egg Pasta (page 83), made into thin lasagne sheets (No.6 on most machines)
900 ml/1 ½ pt Béchamel Sauce (page 9)
60 ml/2 fl oz single cream
1 large onion, sliced
2 cloves garlic, chopped
50 g/2 oz butter
500 g/1 lb boned chicken breasts, cubed

250 g/8 oz mixed oyster, shiitake and field mushrooms, sliced
1 tablespoon tarragon, chopped
salt and freshly ground pepper
50 g/2 oz fresh Parmesan or Pecorino cheese, grated

Boil a few lasagne sheets at a time in a large saucepan of boiling salted water for 1 minute. Fish them out with a flat sieve or slotted spoon and slide them into a large bowl of cold water. Leave for a few seconds, then spread them out on clean tea towels.

Warm the béchamel sauce and stir in the cream.

Heat the onion and garlic gently in the butter until soft, add the chicken and stir over a moderate heat for 5 minutes. Add the mushrooms and tarragon and heat through. Season with salt and pepper and remove from the heat.

Butter a 25 × 18 cm/10 × 7 in ovenproof dish. Spread a thin layer of béchamel sauce over the bottom of the dish, add a layer of the chicken-mushroom mixture, then one of lasagne. Repeat these layers ending with the béchamel. Sprinkle with the Parmesan or Pecorino.**

Heat the oven to 180°C/350°F/Gas Mark 4. Bake for 30 minutes.

** *Can be prepared in advance up to this point.*

Lasagne with Tomato, Courgettes and Basil

SERVES 6

500 g/1 lb Basic Egg Pasta
   (page 83) made into thin
   lasagne sheets
1 large onion, chopped
2 cloves garlic, chopped
50 g/2 oz butter
750 g/1 ½ lb courgettes,
   thinly sliced
3 tablespoons chopped
   basil

salt and freshly ground
   black pepper
900 ml/1 ½ pt Tomato Sauce
   (page 12)
400 g/14 oz mozzarella,
   finely sliced
50 g/2 oz fresh Parmesan
   or Pecorino cheese,
   grated

Boil a few lasagne sheets at a time in a large saucepan of boiling salted water for 1 minute. Fish them out with a flat sieve or slotted spoon and slide them into a large bowl of cold water. Leave for a few seconds, then spread them out on clean tea towels.

Soften the onion and garlic in the butter. Add the courgettes and cook gently until they are limp but not coloured. Remove from the heat and stir in 2 tablespoons of the basil. Season with salt and pepper and leave to cool.

Rub a 25 × 18 cm/10 × 7 in ovenproof dish with oil and make layers starting with the tomato sauce and followed by the pasta and courgettes (using all the juices) and mozzarella. Finish with a layer of the tomato sauce. Sprinkle the top with the Parmesan or Pecorino cheese mixed with the remaining tablespoon of basil and any mozzarella that is left.**

Heat the oven to 180°C/350°F/Gas Mark 4. Bake for 30 minutes.

** *Can be prepared in advance up to this point.*

Pasticcio

In Italy Pasticcio is a baked dish made with pasta and other ingredients bound together with a béchamel or egg sauce. It makes a perfect dinner party entrée, especially this tasty version that includes diced grilled peppers, ham and mozzarella cheese.

SERVES 8

500 g/1 lb dried spinach tagliatelle

900 ml/1 ½ pt Béchamel Sauce (3 × recipe, page 9)

1 tablespoon extra virgin olive oil

4 red peppers, grilled peeled (page 5), seeded and diced

350 g/12 oz thick ham slices, cubed

50 g/2 oz toasted brown breadcrumbs

salt and freshly ground black pepper

450 g/15 oz mozzarella cheese, thinly sliced

150 g/5 oz freshly grated Parmesan cheese

Cook the pasta in a large quantity of boiling salted water until just *al dente* – firm to the bite. Drain it, pour it back into the saucepan and toss with the béchamel, which need only be warm.

Grease a shallow gratin dish with a capacity of approximately 2.5 L/ 4 ½ pt with olive oil. Spread a layer of pasta over the bottom. Cover with a sprinkling of the diced peppers, ham, breadcrumbs, salt and pepper, followed by a layer of mozzarella and some of the grated Parmesan. Repeat these layers until the ingredients are used up, ending with a layer of mozzarella and Parmesan. Cover and refrigerate if you do not plan to eat it within several hours.**

Remove from the refrigerator a few hours before baking if you have used a ceramic baking dish; this will prevent the dish from cracking. Preheat the over to 200°C/400°F/Gas Mark 6.

Cover the dish loosely with foil and bake for 20 minutes. Remove the foil and bake for another 10 minutes. The dish retains its heat for quite a few minutes so there is some scope in serving time.

** *Can be prepared in advance up to this point.*

Spinach and Ricotta Ravioli

No store-bought ravioli can touch the real home-made article – they truly melt in the mouth. It takes a bit of time, but they aren't difficult to make and you will be delighted with the results. Children with their small fingers are particularly adept at it. Ravioli is at its best eaten the same day it is made, but it can be made a day in advance if it is stored between layers of cling film in an airtight box and refrigerated.

SERVES 6

750 g/1½ lb fresh spinach
4 fresh sage leaves, finely
　chopped
250 g/8 oz ricotta cheese
75 g/3 oz boiled ham or
　mortadella, finely
　chopped
salt and freshly ground
　black pepper

500 g/1 lb Basic Egg Pasta
　(page 83)
50 g/2 oz butter
6–8 fresh sage leaves,
　chopped
freshly grated Parmesan
　cheese, to serve

Remove any coarse stalks from the spinach, wash it well and cook it, covered, in the water that is clinging to the leaves, for 5 minutes. Drain and when cool squeeze out as much moisture as you can with your hands. Chop and mix with the sage, ricotta and ham. Season well with salt and pepper.

Make the pasta lengths as thin as possible. Place teaspoons of the stuffing down one side of the pasta rectangle. Fold over the other half and press down gently between the mounds of filling. Cut the dough between the rows with a fluted pastry wheel or a sharp knife to make square ravioli.**

Follow the cooking instructions for Squash Tortellini (page 99).

To make the sauce heat the butter until it foams and turns golden. Add the sage leaves, stir for a few seconds and pour over the pasta. Serve with the Parmesan passed separately.

** *Can be prepared in advance up to this point.*

Squash Tortellini

In Italy pumpkin or squash is often used for stuffing pastas. It was primarily used for fast days. Although these days are officially over, the tradition of this tasty and light pasta remains.

SERVES 4

250 g/8 oz butternut squash, weighed after being peeled and seeded
65 g/2½ oz freshly grated Parmesan cheese
1 amaretti biscuit, crushed (optional)
gratings of nutmeg

salt and freshly ground black pepper
⅔ Basic Egg Pasta (page 83)
semolina
extra virgin olive oil
50 g/2 oz butter, to serve

Cut the squash into chunks and steam it over boiling water for about 12 minutes, or until tender. Drain it into a sieve and shake to get rid of any extra moisture. Turn into a bowl and mash. Add 40 g/ 1½ oz of the Parmesan and the biscuit crumbs. Season well with nutmeg and salt and pepper.

Make the pasta lengths as thin as possible and cut them into 6 cm/ 2½ in rounds with a pastry cutter. Place a small spoonful of the stuffing on the pasta round and fold in half to make a semi-circle. Press the edges together well to seal. Place on clean cloths sprinkled with semolina.**

Bring a large pot of boiling salted water to the boil. Add a few drops of olive oil and slide in the tortellini. Gently boil until tender, 3 to 5 minutes depending on how long they have been drying. Lift out the tortellini with a slotted spoon or Chinese flat sieve. Serve with hot melted butter and the remaining Parmesan.

** *Can be prepared in advance up to this point.*

RISOTTOS & GNOCCHI

Authentic Italian risottos are in a class of their own and can best be achieved with Arborio, Vialono Nono and Carnaroli rice. It absorbs large quantities of liquid which gives the finished risotto a creamy but not mushy texture. The only snag is that the liquid has to be added and stirred in at intervals and the entire process takes about 30 minutes. You don't have to stand over the pot but you do have to keep an eye on it and top up with hot stock as required. The finished results are sumptuous and healthy because there is only a minimum amount of fat used.

Italians serve risotto as a *primo piatto* but it is a substantial dish and need only be followed by a light second course or salad and fruit. Rather like a pasta, the possible ingredients for making risottos are endless. It tastes best, however, when the flavourings are kept to a harmonious few. Whatever the type of risotto you are making the technique is the same. Often finely chopped shallots or onions, or other aromatic vegetables, are softened in oil; the rice is then stirred in and coated in the fat. A small amount of wine or simmering stock is added and when this is absorbed enough stock to cover the rice is poured in. The rice is simmered, uncovered, and ladles of hot stock are added when the rice begins to dry out. Towards the end, the liquid is incorporated in smaller quantities so that the risotto does not dry out but runs no risk of becoming sloppy. The other ingredients are added just to give enough time for them to cook in the rice. The rice is done when it is tender but still firm. The end result should be a creamy, almost pourable mixture.

When it is impractical to cook the rice at the last minute it can be reheated successfully in a microwave.

Basic Risotto

This is a basic risotto recipe. As well as using it with the recipes in this book it can serve as the background for many other ingredients, such as sautéd chicken livers, ham and sage, asparagus or artichoke hearts.

SERVES 4

1 L/1¾ pt stock (chicken, fish or beef depending on other ingredients)
2 tablespoons extra virgin olive oil
50 g/2 oz butter
2 shallots or 1 medium-sized onion, finely chopped

350 g/12 oz Italian risotto rice
splash of dry white wine
salt and freshly ground black pepper
50 g/2 oz freshly grated Parmesan cheese

Heat the stock and keep it at a very low simmer.

Using a heavy-bottomed saucepan, heat the oil with half of the butter and sauté the shallots or onion until soft. Add the rice and stir until it is coated in the fat. Pour in the wine and let it evaporate. Pour in a ladleful of hot stock and stir until the rice absorbs the liquid. Add enough stock to cover the rice and cook over medium heat, stirring occasionally, until this liquid is absorbed. Continue to add ladlefuls of hot stock to the rice, stirring when it has been absorbed to prevent it from sticking to the bottom of the pan. When the rice is nearly cooked – about 25 minutes – stir in whatever cooked ingredients you are using. Season with salt and pepper. Stir in some of the Parmesan cheese and the remaining butter. The rice should be creamy and almost pourable.

Black Risotto

In Venice black risotto is made with cuttlefish which have a large ink sac that is used to colour the rice. Squid are far easier to find here and you can now buy small packets of the ink separately (from enterprising fishmongers), so with this combination it is possible to create a delicious black risotto.

SERVES 4

500 g/1 lb squid, cleaned (page 6)
Basic Risotto (page 101), using fish stock and omitting the Parmesan

2 × 4 g/⅛-oz packets of squid or cuttlefish (calamari or seppie) ink
salt and freshly ground black pepper

Slice the squid sacs into rings and the tentacles into pieces.

Follow the basic risotto recipe, adding the squid after you have sautéd the shallots or onion until soft. When the rice is half cooked, stir in the squid ink. As soon as the rice is done, season with salt and pepper, stir in the remaining butter (omit the cheese) and serve.

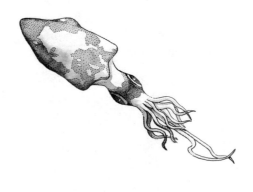

Risotto of Spinach and Sun-dried Tomatoes

Make the Basic Risotto (page 101) and when the rice is nearly cooked follow the recipe below.

SERVES 4–6

250 g/8 oz small- or large-leafed spinach, washed and stalks trimmed

2 tablespoons extra virgin olive oil

125 g/4 oz sun-dried tomatoes, drained and sliced

freshly grated nutmeg

salt and freshly ground black pepper

50 g/2 oz freshly grated Parmesan cheese (optional)

While the rice is cooking, wilt the spinach in a large pan using only the water that is left on the leaves after washing. Drain and gently press out any remaining liquid. Roughly separate the leaves with a fork and leave them to drain on kitchen paper. If you are using the large-leafed spinach, drain it and squeeze out the water, then chop it roughly.

Heat the oil in a pan, stir in the spinach and sun-dried tomatoes and warm them through. Season with the nutmeg, salt and pepper. Add the mixture and half the Parmesan to the rice just before serving. Serve with the remaining Parmesan passed separately.

Squid and Sun-dried Tomato Risotto

Make the Basic Risotto (page 101) and when the rice is nearly cooked follow the instructions below.

SERVES 4–6

25 g/1 oz butter
350 g/12 oz small squid, cleaned (page 6) and sliced into rings, retaining the tentacles

125 g/4 oz sun-dried tomatoes, drained and sliced
salt and freshly ground black pepper

Five minutes before the end of the cooking time for the rice, melt the butter in a heavy-bottomed frying pan and gently cook the squid for 1–2 minutes until it is white and tender.

Remove the rice from the heat, stir in the squid and the sun-dried tomatoes. Season with salt and pepper and serve at once.

Risotto with Radicchio

Radicchio rosso undergoes a transformation when cooked in a risotto. It loses most of its bitterness and turns from red to a mysterious black. In this risotto it is cooked in the rice rather than added at the end.

SERVES 4–6

500 g/1 lb radicchio
Basic Risotto (page 101)

salt and freshly ground black pepper

Separate the radicchio leaves, wash and drain. Stack up several leaves at one time and cut them into narrow strips.

Following the basic risotto recipe, add the radicchio just after you have softened the shallots in the oil and half of the butter. Continue with the recipe until the rice is done – firm but tender, without a chalky centre. The risotto should be creamy and slightly runny. Top up with a bit of hot water if you run out of stock before it is done. Draw the pan off the heat and mix in the rest of the butter and a few tablespoons of the Parmesan. Adjust the seasoning and serve immediately with the remaining Parmesan passed separately.

Blue Cheese Gnocchi with Pepper Sauce

The gnocchi in these recipes are made from baked potatoes instead of the more usual boiled ones. It makes a mixture that tastes less floury and is easier to work with. The potato skins, brushed with olive oil and seasoned with salt and pepper, can be popped back in the oven to crisp up – a delicious cook's perk.

SERVES 4

500 g/1 lb potatoes,
   scrubbed then baked
125 g/4 oz blue cheese,
   crumbled
125 g/4 oz plain flour
1 free-range egg, beaten

salt and freshly ground
   black pepper
450 ml/¾ pt Red Pepper
   Sauce (page 11)
250 g/8 oz mozzarella,
   sliced

Remove the potatoes from the oven and, while they are still hot, scoop out the flesh and mash it finely. Stir in and melt the blue cheese, then add the flour, a little at a time. Mix in the egg, season with salt and pepper, and leave to cool.

With floured hands break off pieces of the dough and form cylindrical rolls about 2.5 cm/1 in thick. Cut the rolls into 2.5 cm/1 in lengths. Lay the gnocchi on trays covered with kitchen cloths. Poach them in gently boiling salted water for 5–7 minutes. Remove with a slotted spoon and drain on kitchen paper.**

Heat the oven to 180°C/350°F/Gas Mark 4.

Butter a large ovenproof dish and lay the gnocchi in it, then cover them with the warmed pepper sauce and spread the slices of mozzarella or top. Bake for 20 minutes or until hot and bubbling.

** *Can be prepared in advance up to this point.*

Potato Gnocchi in Tomato Sauce

SERVES 4

500 g/1 lb large baking
  potatoes
25 g/1 oz butter
1 free-range egg
75–100 g/3 3 ½ oz plain flour
50 g/2 oz freshly grated
  Parmesan cheese, plus
  extra to serve

a few gratings of nutmeg
1 tablespoon sunflower oil
900 ml/1 ½ pt Tomato Sauce
  (page 12)
salt and freshly ground
  black pepper

Preheat the oven to 200°C/400°F/Gas Mark 6 and bake the potatoes for 1 hour, or until very tender. Holding them with an oven glove, cut the potatoes in half and scoop the insides into a shallow bowl. This will allow some of the steam to evaporate and will help dry the potatoes. While the potatoes are still hot, purée them with a potato masher or food mill. Beat in the butter and egg. Sift the flour and beat in just enough to make a dough that is soft and smooth and just slightly sticky. Beat in the grated Parmesan and the nutmeg. Season with salt and pepper. Leave to cool.

With floured hands break off pieces of the dough and form sausage-like rolls about 2.5 cm/1 in thick. Cut the rolls into 2.5 cm/1 in lengths. With a fork gently dent the middles of the gnocchi to help them to cook evenly. Lay the gnocchi on trays covered with kitchen cloths.**

Bring a large quantity of water to the boil, add 1 tablespoon of salt and the sunflower oil. Cook the gnocchi very gently for 10–12 minutes. Do not overcook or they will fall apart. Lift them out with a slotted spoon or flat Chinese sieve, and place on a heated serving dish. Pour the sauce over them and serve with some grated Parmesan passed separately.

** *Can be prepared in advance up to this point.*

PIZZAS

When pizzas are home-made they can reach unsuspected heights of culinary glory and provide an exciting colourful meal-in-one or first course. They are so good that once you have made your own pizza you will never be happy with commercial ones again. If you take to making them regularly, invest in a pizza paddle and stone. The stone will give the pizza a very crunchy bottom crust and the paddle will enable you, with very little practice, to slide the pizza on to the hot stone with ease.

*** Can be prepared in advance up to this point.*

Pizza Dough

SUFFICIENT FOR TWO 27–30 cm/11–12 in PIZZAS

7 g/¼ oz fresh yeast or 1
   teaspoon of dried yeast
125 g/4 fl oz warm water
200 g/7 oz plain or strong
   white flour

½ teaspoon salt
1 tablespoon extra virgin
   olive oil

Place the yeast in the warm water and leave to dissolve. Turn the flour and salt into a bowl, make a well in the centre and add the yeasty water and olive oil. Stir until the mixture forms a mass. Turn the dough out on to a floured board and knead until soft and smooth, adding a bit more flour if the dough is too sticky. Place in a greased bowl, cover with a damp cloth and leave to rise in a warm place for at least 30 minutes.

Place a baking sheet or pizza stone in the centre of the oven and preheat the oven to 230°C/450°F/Gas Mark 8.

When the dough has risen, punch it down and divide it into two balls. (Freeze one ball for future use if you are making only one pizza.) Roll out from the centre into rounds about 30 cm/12 in in diameter. Place on a floured board or pizza paddle and turn the edges up slightly. Cover with a cloth and leave until the oven is hot.

Cover with the topping and slide on to the baking sheet or pizza stone. Bake for 15 minutes.

Wholemeal Pizza Dough

Follow the recipe for the basic pizza dough but substitute wholemeal flour for one-third of the white flour. Add a little milk if necessary to make a soft, smooth dough.

Note: If you are short of time, increase the yeast by half which will reduce the rising time to about 15 minutes.

Aubergine, Pesto and Caramelized Onion Pizza

One pizza should be enough for two as the main course. If you are making more than one pizza you can half-bake the first, pull it out of the oven and bake the second, then finish off the first while you start eating the second! Sounds complicated but it works very well and any number of pizzas can be half-baked and then finished off while you eat.

SERVES 2 AS MAIN COURSE AND 3–4 AS STARTER

4 tablespoons extra virgin olive oil, plus extra

500 g/1 lb onions, quartered then finely sliced

2 small aubergines, finely sliced

½ Pizza Dough recipe (page 108)

2 tablespoons Pesto (page 10)

250 g/8 oz Feta cheese, crumbled

salt and freshly ground black pepper

Heat 2 tablespoons of olive oil in a heavy frying pan and cook the onions over a low heat for 30 minutes until they have caramelized.**

Preheat the oven to 230°C/450°F/Gas Mark 8 and put a heavy baking sheet or pizza stone in to heat.

Heat the grill or ridged cast-iron grill pan to a high temperature. Brush the aubergine slices with the remaining olive oil and brown both sides.

Spread the onions over the pizza base, stopping 1 cm/½ in from the edge. Brush the aubergine slices with pesto and lay them on top of the onions. Scatter on the crumbled Feta, drizzle over a little olive oil and season with salt and pepper. Slide the pizza on to the baking tray or stone. Cook for 15 minutes, until the topping is bubbling. Serve immediately.

** *Can be prepared in advance up to this point.*

Onion, Anchovy, Tomato and Olive Pizza

MAKE A 27–30 cm/11–12 in PIZZA

extra virgin olive oil
500 g/1 lb onions,
   quartered, then finely
   sliced
½ Pizza Dough recipe
   (page 108)
250 g/8 oz tomatoes,
   skinned, seeded and
   chopped

1 tin of anchovies, drained
   and chopped
12 Kalamata olives
salt and freshly ground
   black pepper
1 tablespoon chopped basil,
   to serve

Preheat the oven to 230°C/450°F/Gas Mark 8 and put a heavy baking sheet or pizza stone in to heat.

Heat 2 tablespoons of olive oil in a heavy-bottomed frying pan and cook the onions over a low heat, stirring occasionally, until they have caramelized.**

Spread the onions over the pizza base, stopping 1 cm/½ in from the edge, followed by the tomatoes and anchovies. Dot on the olives and season with salt and pepper. Drizzle on a little extra olive oil.

Slide the pizza on to the baking tray or stone. Cook for 15 minutes, until the topping is bubbling. Sprinkle the basil over the pizza and serve.

** *Can be prepared in advance up to this point.*

Red Pepper, Anchovy and Smoked Mozzarella Pizza

MAKES A 27–30 cm/11–12 in PIZZA

450 ml/¾ pt Red Pepper
  Sauce (page 11), reduced
  to a firm purée**
½ Pizza Dough recipe
  (page 108)
125 g/4 oz smoked
  mozzarella, sliced thinly

12 Kalamata olives
salt and freshly ground
  black pepper
50 g/2 oz tin of anchovies

Preheat the oven to 230°C/450°F/Gas Mark 8 and put a heavy baking sheet or pizza stone in to heat.

Spread the pepper purée evenly over the pizza base, stopping 1 cm/½ in from the edge. Drain the anchovies and lay them in lines on top of the pepper purée with the mozzarella slices in between. Dot with the olives and season with salt and pepper.

Slide the pizza on to the baking tray or stone. Bake for 15 minutes until the mozzarella is golden and the top is bubbling. Serve immediately.

** *Can be prepared in advance up to this point.*

Sun-dried Tomato and Mozzarella Pizza

MAKES A 27–30 cm/11–12 in PIZZA

900 ml/1 ½ pt Tomato Sauce
   (page 12)
2 tablespoons chopped
   basil
½ Pizza Dough recipe
   (page 108)
200 g/7 oz sun-dried
   tomatoes, drained and
   sliced

125 g/4 oz mozzarella,
   sliced
12 Kalamata olives
salt and freshly ground
   black pepper

Preheat the oven to 230°C/450°F/Gas Mark 8 and put a shallow baking tray or pizza stone in to heat.

Simmer the tomato sauce, uncovered, until it is a thick purée.** Mix 1 tablespoon of the chopped basil into the tomato purée and spread it over the pizza base, stopping 1 cm/½ in from the edge. Lay the sun-dried tomato and mozzarella slices on the top. Dot on the olives and season with salt and pepper.

Slide the pizza on to the baking tray or stone. Cook for 15 minutes, until the mozzarella is golden and the top is bubbling. Sprinkle the remaining basil over the pizza and serve immediately.

** *Can be prepared in advance up to this point.*

Wild Mushroom and Fontina Pizza

Wild mushrooms have such good flavour that even a very few lift the cultivated varieties.

MAKES A 27–30 cm/11–12 in PIZZA

125 g/4 oz wild mushrooms, such as porcini, chanterelles, horns of plenty or fairy ring

175 g/6 oz oyster mushrooms

4 tablespoons extra virgin olive oil, plus extra

1–2 cloves garlic, finely chopped

2 tablespoons chopped parsley

salt and freshly ground black pepper

250 g/8 oz Fontina cheese, sliced

½ Pizza Dough recipe (page 108)

Preheat the oven to 230°C/450°F/Gas Mark 8 and put a shallow baking sheet or pizza stone in to heat.

Wipe the wild mushrooms clean with a damp cloth, then slice them, along with the oyster mushrooms. Heat the olive oil in a heavy-bottomed frying pan and stir in the mushrooms, garlic, parsley and some salt. Cook until the mushrooms have softened.**

Make a layer of the mushrooms and Fontina slices on the pizza base, season with salt and pepper and drizzle a little olive oil over the top. Slide the pizza on to the baking tray or stone. Cook for 15 minutes, until the Fontina is melted and bubbling. Serve at once.

VARIATION:
Substitute 40 g/1½ oz dried porcini for the fresh wild mushrooms. Soak them in boiling water for 30 minutes. Rub off any grit under cold running water, then slice and cook with the oyster mushrooms, using some of the filtered soaking water.

** *Can be prepared in advance up to this point.*

SAVOURY TARTS

Mixed Fish Tart

Any mixture of boned fish can be used in this tart and, if your budget allows, even a few queen scallops instead of, or as well as, the prawns.

SERVES 6–8

500 g/1 lb mixed filleted
  fish – undyed smoked
  haddock, cod, monkfish,
  salmon
2 tablespoons extra virgin
  olive oil
1 clove garlic, crushed
salt and freshly ground
  black pepper

3 large free-range eggs
250 ml/8 fl oz single cream
$\frac{1}{4}$ teaspoon ground mace
1 tablespoon chopped
  parsley
125 g/4 oz peeled prawns
23–25-cm/9–10-in
  Shortcrust Pastry case,
  baked blind (page 19)

Heat the oven to 180°C/350°F/Gas Mark 4.

Skin the fish and cut it into 2.5-cm/1-in cubes. Heat the oil and garlic in a large heavy-bottomed frying pan, then add the fish. Stir over a gentle heat for 3–4 minutes, season with salt and pepper and remove from the heat.**

Beat the eggs and cream together, season with mace, salt and pepper, and stir in the parsley. Place the fish and prawns in the pastry case and pour the egg mixture over the top.

Bake in the oven for 25–30 minutes until it is just setting. Cool slightly before removing from the tin and serve warm.

** *Can be prepared in advance up to this point.*

Gruyère and Tomato Tart

A savoury tomato and cheese tart that contains no eggs.

SERVES 6–8

Shortcrust Pastry (page 19)
6–7 medium-sized good-
  flavoured tomatoes
50 g/2 oz tin of anchovies,
  drained
125 ml/4 fl oz double
  cream

175 g/6 oz Gruyère cheese,
  grated
50 g/2 oz brown
  breadcrumbs
$\frac{1}{2}$ teaspoon dried thyme
salt and freshly ground
  black pepper

Roll out the pastry and line a 23 cm/9 in flan tin with a removable base. Chill the shell while you are making the filling.

Set a baking sheet in the middle of the oven and preheat to 200°C/400°F/Gas Mark 6.

Drop 1 or 2 tomatoes at a time into simmering water, leave for 30 seconds, retrieve with a slotted spoon and peel off the skins as soon as they are cool enough to handle. Cut in half and remove the seeds using your fingers. Cut out the dark stem base.

Mash or finely chop the anchovies and mix with the cream. Stir in the cheese to make a very thick mixture.** Place the breadcrumbs in the base of the tart. Arrange the tomatoes in a layer over the crumbs. Season with the thyme, salt and pepper. Spoon the cheese mixture in between and over the tomatoes.

Bake for 30 minutes, until the top is bubbling and brown. Allow to cool for 10 minutes before serving.

** *Can be prepared in advance up to this point.*

Leek and Bacon Tart

Crisp well-flavoured winter leeks combined with bacon make this an excellent tart for colder days.

SERVES 6

1 medium onion, sliced
2 cloves garlic, chopped
250 g/8 oz streaky bacon,
    cut into 1 cm/½ in pieces
50 g/2 oz butter
500 g/1 lb leeks, finely
    sliced
2 tablespoons chopped
    parsley

salt and freshly ground
    black pepper
4 free-range eggs
250 ml/8 fl oz single cream
½ nutmeg, grated
23–25 cm/9–10 in
    Shortcrust Pastry case,
    baked blind (page 19)

Heat the oven to 180°C/350°F/Gas Mark 4.

Soften the onion, garlic and bacon in the butter, add the leeks and cook them slowly for about 5 minutes until they have wilted. Remove from the heat and stir in the parsley. Season with pepper and a little salt depending on the saltiness of the bacon.**

Beat together the eggs and cream. Season and add the grated nutmeg. Mix the leeks into the egg mixture and pour it into the pastry case.

Bake for 30 minutes until it is just setting. Serve warm.

** *Can be prepared in advance up to this point.*

Flamiche of Leeks

A flamiche is a French version of Italian calzone but made with puff pastry instead of pizza dough. It is a versatile wrapping for many combinations of ingredients.

SERVES 4

1 medium onion, finely
   sliced
125 g/4 oz butter
350 g/12 oz leeks, washed
   and finely sliced
1 egg yolk

125 ml/4 fl oz double cream
salt and freshly ground
   black pepper
250 g/8 oz Puff Pastry
   (page 18)
beaten egg or milk

Soften the onion in half of the butter, then add the leeks and the remaining butter. Cook gently for about 5 minutes until the leeks have wilted. Turn up the heat to evaporate the juices but do not allow the vegetables to brown. Mix the egg yolk into the cream and pour it over the leeks, heat through for 1 minute, season with salt and pepper. Leave to cool.**

Heat the oven to 200°C/400°F/Gas Mark 6.

Roll the pastry out into a rectangle and spread the leek mixture over one half. Fold the other half over the top and seal the edges with a little milk. Brush the pastry with beaten egg or milk.

Place in the oven on a baking tray for 10 minutes, then reduce the heat to 180°C/350°F/Gas Mark 4 and bake for a further 20 minutes. Serve in slices with a green salad.

VARIATIONS:
Use 500 g/1 lb onions, cooked in butter until golden with 250 g/8 oz cooked diced ham or gammon, instead of the leeks.

Replace the leeks with 250 g/8 oz mixed mushrooms, wild or cultivated or a mixture of both.

** *Can be prepared in advance up to this point.*

Onion Tart with Anchovies and Olives

There are many versions of onion tart – this one has the same main ingredients as a Pissaladière (page 76), but it is set with eggs and cream into a luscious filling.

SERVES 6

2 tablespoons extra virgin
    olive oil
750 g/1 ½ lb red onions,
    quartered and finely
    sliced
2 cloves garlic, chopped
75 g/3 oz Kalamata olives,
    stoned and chopped

4 free-range eggs
250 ml/8 fl oz single cream
salt and freshly ground
    black pepper
23–25-cm/9–10-in Olive Oil
    Pastry case, baked blind
    (page 17)
1 tin of anchovies

Heat the oven to 180°C/350°F/Gas Mark 4.

Heat the oil in a large heavy-bottomed frying pan and cook the onions for about 20 minutes over a low heat until they are soft. If necessary, turn up the heat briefly to caramelize them. Remove from the heat and stir in the garlic and olives.**

Beat together the eggs and cream, season with salt and pepper and stir in the onions. Pour the mixture into the pastry case.

Bake for 20 minutes until just beginning to set, then lay the drained anchovy strips over the top. Replace in the oven for a further 10 minutes and serve warm.

** *Can be prepared in advance up to this point.*

Mixed Pepper Tart

Peppers are particularly successful as tart fillings. The most succulent are the red and yellow varieties. The green are useful occasionally for a contrast of colour but they do not have the flavour of the other colours. In this tart the peppers are baked with onion, olives and cheese, and scented with basil.

SERVES 6

4 tablespoons extra virgin olive oil
2 red peppers, thinly sliced
1 orange or yellow pepper, thinly sliced
1 onion, finely sliced
2 cloves garlic, chopped
60 ml/2 fl oz white wine
salt and freshly ground black pepper
1 generous handful of basil leaves, chopped

2 tablespoons fresh Parmesan or Pecorino cheese, grated
3 free-range eggs
250 ml/8 fl oz single cream
23–25-cm/9–10-in Shortcrust Pastry case, baked blind (page 19)
20 Kalamata olives
125 g/4 oz Cheddar mature cheese, grated

Heat 2 tablespoons of the oil in a large frying pan and add the peppers, onion and garlic. Stir together for a few minutes, then pour in the wine. Cover and cook gently until the peppers are soft, about 20 minutes. Season with salt and pepper and remove from the heat.** Mix the remaining oil into the basil and Parmesan cheese and add it to the pepper mixture.

Heat the oven to 180°C/350°F/Gas Mark 4.

Beat the eggs and cream together and season with salt and pepper. Spread the peppers over the pastry case and dot with the olives. Pour the egg mixture over the top.

Bake in the oven for 20 minutes until it is just beginning to set. Sprinkle the Cheddar over the tart and return it to the oven for a further 10 minutes. Serve warm.

** *Can be prepared in advance up to this point.*

Ricotta and Basil Tart

A tart to cook in the summer when basil and parsley are plentiful. Ricotta needs to be eaten as fresh as possible so find out when it is delivered to your delicatessen or, if you can only find it packaged in supermarkets, check that there is still plenty of time before the expiry date.

SERVES 6

75 g/3 oz fresh basil leaves
40 g/1½ oz flat-leafed
  parsley
125 ml/4 fl oz extra virgin
  olive oil
salt and coarsely crushed
  black pepper
875 g/1¾ lb fresh ricotta
  cheese

2 eggs plus 1 extra egg
  yolk
50 g/2 oz freshly grated
  Parmesan
16 Kalamata olives, stoned
23–25-cm/9–10-in
  Shortcrust Pastry case,
  baked blind (page 19)

Heat the oven to 180°C/350°F/Gas Mark 4.

Place the basil, parsley and olive oil in the food processor and blend together. Season well with salt and pepper. Turn the ricotta out into a large bowl. Whisk the eggs in a separate bowl and very gently fold them into the ricotta, using a large metal spoon. Fold in the Parmesan. It makes a lot of difference to the final tart if you keep the mixture as light and airy as possible. Fold in the basil mixture and the olives and check the seasoning. Pour the filling into the pastry case and bake for 30–35 minutes. Serve warm.

FISH

Brill with Mushrooms and Coriander

This is an excellent and trouble-free method of cooking fish. The fish is placed on a little white wine or fish stock in the grill pan and grilled over high heat. It doesn't have to be turned and the steam generated by the wine helps to keep it moist and gives it flavour. Brill is a beautiful fish – as superior as Dover sole and cheaper.

SERVES 4

2 × 750 g/1½ lb brill, filleted and bones retained
(bouquet garni)
6 peppercorns
seasoning
500 g/1 lb button mushrooms, finely sliced
2 tablespoons extra virgin olive oil
¼ teaspoon harissa sauce
10 tablespoons (1 large bunch) chopped coriander leaves
grated rind of 1 lime
3 tablespoons mascarpone cheese or crème fraîche

Rinse the fish bones (including heads) in cold water. Chop and place them in a saucepan with the bouquet garni and peppercorns. Cover with cold water. Bring slowly to the boil, skimming occasionally, and simmer for 25 minutes, uncovered. Strain and season to taste.

Sauté the mushrooms in the oil until lightly cooked. Season with salt and pepper. Stir in the harissa, coriander and lime rind.**

Heat the grill. Pour the fish stock to a depth of 3 mm/⅛ in in the grill pan. Lay the fish on top, skin side down. Brush with olive oil and season with salt and pepper. Grill for 3–4 minutes, depending on the thickness of the fillets.

While the fish is cooking, add the mascarpone or crème fraîche to the mushrooms and heat through. Serve the fillets with a mound of the coriander mushrooms.

** *Can be prepared in advance up to this point.*

Baked Cod with Aïoli and Spring Greens

Rather than baked, the cod can be poached or microwaved. The spring greens can be replaced by spinach or chard. Serve this dish with mashed potatoes made with olive oil.

SERVES 4

4 thick fresh cod steaks, skinned	salt and freshly ground black pepper
1 tablespoon extra virgin olive oil	500 g/1 lb spring greens Aïoli (page 15)**

Heat the oven to 150°C/300°F/Gas Mark 2.

Brush the cod steaks with oil and lightly season. Place them in slightly roomy parcels made with pieces of foil or greaseproof paper and crimp the edges to seal. Set the parcels on a baking sheet and bake for 15–20 minutes.

Wash the greens and remove any coarse stalks. Cut the greens into thin strips and place them in a saucepan with some salt and just enough water to cover the bottom of the pan. Cook, covered, until the greens are wilted and barely tender, about 4 minutes.

Serve the cod on a bed of greens with the Aïoli and the mashed potatoes: for this, don't use butter but add 3 tablespoons of extra virgin olive oil to 125 ml/4 fl oz full cream milk, and slowly add to the potatoes as you mash them.

** Can be prepared in advance up to this point.

Cod with a Herb Crust

This is simplicity itself. The usual breadcrumb coating is mixed with fresh herbs and their flavour adds a surprising new dimension.

SERVES 4

750g/1 ½ lb fresh cod fillets, skinned

75 g/3 oz fresh breadcrumbs

3 tablespoons mixed fresh herbs, including tarragon, thyme and parsley, finely chopped

salt and freshly ground black pepper

1 egg, lightly beaten

4 tablespoons extra virgin olive oil

25 g/1 oz butter

lemon wedges, to serve

To remove the skin from the cod, lay it, skin side down, on a chopping board, place a knife with the blade at an angle under the edge of the skin and resting on the board. Pull the skin with your fingers with one hand while you hold the knife firm with the other. The skin will peel away easily. If the fish is very fresh you can peel off the skin just using your fingers.

Mix the breadcrumbs with the herbs and season with salt and pepper. Season the beaten egg. Moisten the fillets in the egg and then roll them in the herb crumbs. Heat the oil and butter together, add the fish and sauté on both sides until the breadcrumbs are nicely browned, about 5 minutes on each side depending on the thickness of the fish. Serve with wedges of lemon.

Cod with Onion and Black Olive Confit

With the confit made in advance you can choose between grilling the fish or baking it to complete the dish in minutes. Both are simple and quick to do, so this is an easy dish to serve if you are entertaining. The confit goes well with other fish such as tuna or swordfish that are particularly good grilled.

SERVES 4

750 g/1½ lb onions, finely sliced
350 ml/12 fl oz dry white wine
salt and freshly ground black pepper
2 teaspoons soft brown sugar

10 Kalamata olives, stoned and chopped
2 tablespoons chopped parsley
4 × 175g/6 oz cod steaks, 2 cm/¾ in thick
extra virgin olive oil

Place the onions in a large pan and pour in the wine. Cover and simmer for 1½–2 hours until the onions are very soft. Season with salt and pepper and add the brown sugar. Continue to cook, uncovered, until the liquid has evaporated. Stir in the olives and half the parsley.** Keep the confit warm if you will be using it immediately.

Heat the grill or ridged cast-iron grill pan to maximum temperature. Brush the cod with olive oil and season with salt and pepper. Grill each side for 2–3 minutes. Serve garnished with the remaining parsley and the warm confit.

Alternatively, preheat the oven to 200°C/400°F/Gas Mark 6. Make a layer of confit in a shallow ovenproof dish. Place the fish in one layer on top. Brush with olive oil and bake for 10 minutes. Sprinkle the parsley on the fish and serve.

** *Can be prepared in advance up to this point.*

Crab Cakes with Creamed Lentils

Good fishmongers cook and dress crabs daily. As there is little difference in the price of fresh or frozen crabmeat it is well worth finding a reliable source.

SERVES 4

Lentil Purée with Crème Fraîche (page 188)
1 medium potato, baked or boiled and drained
250 g/8 oz fresh white crabmeat
125 g/4 oz cod fillet, lightly poached
2 tablespoons chopped coriander
1 free-range egg or 2 yolks
salt and freshly ground black pepper
25 g/1 oz butter
2 tablespoons extra virgin olive oil

While the lentils are cooking prepare the crab cakes. Sieve the potato into a bowl and add the crabmeat, cod and coriander. Bind with the egg and season. Form the crab cakes into small rounds.**

When the lentils are ready, heat the butter and oil in a heavy-bottomed frying pan and fry the cakes for 2–3 minutes on each side until they are golden.

Divide the hot lentils between four plates, place the crab cakes on the top and serve.

** Can be prepared in advance up to this point.

Fish Stew with Aïoli

Buy fish on the bone and ask the fishmonger to fillet it and give you the bones as well as some extra bones and heads from white fish. They are usually supplied free and will make a delicious fish stock for the basis of this soup.

SERVES 4–6

1.25 kg/3 lb (boned weight) mixed white fish, such as cod, haddock, monkfish, sea bass, halibut or John Dory, filleted and bones retained

2 tablespoons extra virgin olive oil

1 onion, chopped

2 leeks, sliced

1 fennel bulb, chopped, with greens retained and chopped

1 bay leaf

several sprigs of fresh parsley and dill or chervil

1.5 L/2½ pt water

salt

125 ml/4 fl oz dry white wine

250 g/8 oz mixed shellfish, such as scallops, mussels or prawns

freshly ground black pepper

175 ml/6 fl oz Aïoli (page 15)

Cut the fish into 2.5-cm/1-in cubes and set aside.

Heat the oil in a large saucepan and sauté the vegetables gently until they have softened. Rinse the fish bones in cold water. Add the bones, bay leaf and herbs to the vegetables and pour in the water. Salt lightly and bring to the boil. Skim any scum from the surface and simmer for 20 minutes. Pour in the wine and continue to cook for 10 minutes. Remove from the heat and strain.** Put the fish into a large saucepan and cover with the fish stock. Bring to the boil and add the shellfish. Simmer, covered, until any that are in their shells have opened, about 2–3 minutes, then remove from the heat. Check the seasoning and add the pepper. Lift the fish and shellfish out with a slotted spoon and place in a large heated soup tureen.

Put half of the aïoli aside to serve with the fish. Place a tablespoonful of the remaining aïoli into a small bowl, and whisk a ladleful of the fish stock into it. Whisk in the rest of the aïoli and a little more stock until you have a smooth mixture, then tip it back into the pan and reheat gently. Do not allow it to come near boiling point.

** *Can be prepared in advance up to this point.*

Pour the soup over the fish and sprinkle with the chopped fennel greens. Serve with the retained aïoli.

VARIATION:
Use a mixture of small whole fish such as red snapper or grey mullet. Allow 350–400 g/12–14 oz per person. Make the stock as above, using white fish bones from the fishmonger, and add to it 500 g/1 lb tomatoes, skinned, seeded and chopped, garlic, paprika and cayenne pepper. Cook the fish for 5–10 minutes before adding stronger flavoured shellfish such as prawns or mussels. Replace the Aïoli with Rouille (page 15).

** Can be prepared in advance up to this point.

Monkfish with Peppers and Tomato Sauce

With the tomato sauce prepared in advance, the final assembling takes only a few minutes and the dish can be baked while you are eating your first course.

SERVES 6

250 g/8 oz onions, finely
  sliced
3 tablespoons extra virgin
  olive oil
750 g/1½ lb ripe tomatoes,
  skinned, seeded and
  chopped
4 cloves garlic, chopped
salt and freshly ground
  black pepper
6 × 200–250 g/7–8 oz
  monkfish cutlets on the
  bone or tail fillets

2 red peppers, or 1 red and
  1 yellow, grilled, peeled
  (page 5), seeded and
  finely sliced

To serve:
1 tablespoon chopped
  parsley
grated rind of 1 well-
  scrubbed or unwaxed
  lemon

Sweat the onions in 2 tablespoons of oil in a covered pan over a low heat for about 20 minutes. Add the tomatoes and continue to cook very slowly for a further 20 minutes. Add the garlic and season with salt and pepper. **

Heat the oven to 200°C/400°F/Gas Mark 6.

Season the fish with salt and pepper and brush it with the remaining oil. Heat a large heavy-bottomed frying pan and sear the cutlets for 2–3 minutes on each side depending on the thickness of the fish.

Place the fish in an oiled ovenproof dish, lay the slices of pepper on top and cover with the tomato sauce. Bake in the oven for 10–15 minutes. Mix together the parsley and lemon rind and sprinkle them over the fish before serving.

** *Can be prepared in advance up to this point.*

Monkfish with Tomatoes and Oyster Mushrooms

Monkfish tails can shrink during baking so the amount you will need is slightly more than normal. Allow 250g/8 oz per person on the bone and 175g/6 oz for filleted fish.

SERVES 4–6

1 kg/2 lb tomatoes, peeled, seeded and chopped
2 cloves garlic, chopped
3 tablespoons chopped parsley
6 tablespoons extra virgin olive oil
salt and freshly ground black pepper
1 pinch of sugar
250 g/8 oz oyster mushrooms, sliced
125 ml/4 fl oz crème fraîche
1-1.5 kg/2-3 lb monkfish tail or 2 smaller ones

Simmer the tomatoes, garlic, 2 tablespoons of parsley and 2 table-spoons of olive oil together until it becomes a thick purée, about 15–20 minutes. Season with salt and pepper and a pinch of sugar if necessary.

Using a frying pan, briefly sauté the mushrooms in 2 tablespoons of olive oil. Mix them into the tomato purée, followed by the crème fraîche. Season with salt and pepper.**

Meanwhile, heat the oven to 200°C/400/Gas Mark 6.

Put the fish in an oiled ovenproof dish and drizzle the remaining 2 tablespoons of olive oil over the top. Season with salt and pepper.

Place in the oven for 15 minutes, then pour in 60 ml/2 fl oz of water. Turn the heat down to 150°C/300°F/Gas Mark 2 for a further 15 minutes (10 for 2 small tails) and baste occasionally. Pour the warm sauce over the fish and bake for another 5 minutes. Serve with the remaining parsley scattered over the top.

** Can be prepared in advance up to this point.

Grilled Salmon with Tomatoes and Basil

John Dory, when available, is also delicious cooked to this recipe, or for a cheaper alternative use cod or haddock. When grilling fish the heat source should be very hot so the fish can sear quickly and seal in the juices. Fish cooks incredibly fast and it will continue to cook when taken off the heat so keep it on the underdone side.

SERVES 4

4 tablespoons extra virgin olive oil
2 shallots, finely diced
500 g/1 lb ripe tomatoes, peeled, seeded and chopped
50 g/2 oz sun-dried tomatoes, sliced finely

salt and freshly ground black pepper
4 × 175 g/6 oz salmon fillets cut from the thick end and skinned
2 tablespoons chopped basil

Heat 2 tablespoons of the oil and gently fry the shallots until they are soft but not coloured. Add the tomatoes, warm them through, then stir in the sun-dried tomatoes. Season with salt and pepper, remove from the heat and keep warm.

Heat the grill or ridged cast-iron grill pan to maximum temperature.

Brush both sides of the salmon fillets with the remaining oil and season with salt and pepper.

Grill the salmon very quickly – about 3 minutes on each side should be sufficient, depending on the thickness of the fish.

Stir the basil into the warm sauce and spoon it over the salmon fillets.

Salmon Steaks with Anchoïade

If you can find nice thick boneless salmon steaks this recipe will make the most of them. They will cook in the time it takes to clear the first course dishes if your grill is preheated. (Even guests who aren't anchovy fans have been enthusiastic.) It is also good with the more economical unboned slices but less sensational. Serve with baked or grilled vegetables (page 59 or 60).

SERVES 8

2 × 50 g/2 oz tins of anchovy fillets
1–2 cloves garlic, finely chopped
2 teaspoons cider vinegar
5–6 tablespoon extra virgin olive oil
salt and freshly ground black pepper

250 ml/8 fl oz dry white wine
8 × 150–175 g/5–6 oz thick salmon slices cut from the thick end of a filleted fish (about 4 cm/ 1 ½ in thick)

Drain the anchovies and chop finely. Place in a mortar with the garlic and vinegar and mash together slightly. Gradually stir in the olive oil and season with pepper. Set aside.**

Heat the grill, timing it so it is good and hot when you plan to cook the fish. Pour the wine into the grill pan, place the fish on top and lightly season. Grill for 5–8 minutes, depending on the thickness of the fish. Spoon a thin layer of the anchovy sauce over the top of the fish and serve.

** Can be prepared in advance up to this point.

Salmon in Pastry with Herb Sauce

This dish makes an impressive main course for a party and can be prepared 4–6 hours in advance if refrigerated. A salmon of about 2.75 kg/6 lb will feed about twelve people. For that size just double the amount of pastry and increase the stuffing and sauce by half. Add another 10 minutes of baking time. Check first that your oven is large enough to take the bigger fish.

SERVES 6

1.25 kg/2½ lb salmon, filleted and skinned
salt and freshly ground black pepper
75 g/3 oz butter, softened
1 bunch of chives, chopped
1 tablespoon chopped parsley
1 tablespoon chopped chervil, tarragon or marjoram
1½ Shortcrust Pastry (page 19)
1 egg yolk mixed with 1 tablespoon of cream and 1 pinch of salt, to glaze

For the sauce:
2 shallots, chopped
50 g/2 oz butter
5 tablespoons chopped mixed herbs, such as parsley, chervil, marjoram, tarragon
1 teaspoon Dijon mustard
1 teaspoon flour
125 ml/4 fl oz dry white wine
125 ml/4 fl oz crème fraîche
2 egg yolks mixed with 1 tablespoon cream

Season the salmon fillets with salt and pepper. Mix together the butter and herbs, and season. Spread the mixture over one of the fillets and place the other fillet on top.

Divide the pastry into two slightly unequal pieces – roll out the smaller piece of pastry into a rectangle 5 cm/2 in larger than the fish. Place the pastry on an oiled baking tray and lay the fish on top. Roll out the second piece of pastry until it is about 2.5 cm/1 in larger than the first and place it on top of the fish. Press the edges together, trim off any surplus and pinch the edges together to seal them. Decorate with the trimmings. Leave in the fridge until just before cooking.**

Preheat the oven to 220°C/425°F/Gas Mark 7. Brush the pastry with the glaze and place in the oven for 30 minutes.

** *Can be prepared in advance up to this point.*

While the fish is cooking, soften the shallots in the butter but do not allow them to colour. Add the herbs and stir in the mustard and flour. Cook for 1 minute, then slowly add the wine. Simmer gently for 5 minutes, stirring frequently, then add the crème fraîche followed by the egg yolks. Continue to stir over gentle heat until the sauce thickens. Do not allow it to come near boiling point. Keep warm in a bain-marie.

Slide the fish on to a heated platter. Serve in slices with the sauce passed separately.

VARIATION:
Spread seasoned butter on the bottom fillet and cover with precooked asparagus tips – all facing in the same direction. Serve with the sauce above or Green Mayonnaise (page 15).

Baked Skate with Balsamic Vinegar, Capers and Olive Oil

This is a lighter and healthier way of serving skate compared to the traditional *beurre noir* with which it is usually associated.

SERVES 4

1.25–1.5 kg/2½–3 lb skate wings, cut into 4 pieces
salt and freshly ground black pepper
5 tablespoons extra virgin olive oil
2–3 tablespoons balsamic vinegar

2 tablespoons capers, rinsed
1 tablespoon finely chopped parsley, to serve

Heat the oven to 190°C/375°F/Gas Mark 5.

Pat the skate dry and season lightly with salt and pepper. Arrange in an oiled gratin dish large enough to contain the fish in one layer. Sprinkle with the olive oil, vinegar and capers. Cover with foil** and bake for 15 minutes.

Serve the fish basted with the juices and sprinkled with parsley.

** *Can be prepared in advance up to this point.*

Squid Baked in Garlic

Good country bread and a green salad are all that are needed to accompany this robustly flavoured dish. It is best cooked when the new season's garlic is still pearly white, plump and juicy.

SERVES 4

16 × 10-cm/4-in squid, cleaned (page 6)
8 cloves garlic, chopped
2 tablespoons extra virgin olive oil
2 tablespoons dry white wine

salt and freshly ground black pepper
175 g/6 oz mixed small salad leaves, including rocket
2 tablespoons chopped parsley, to serve

Heat the oven to 220°C/425°F/Gas Mark 7.

Toss the squid in a bowl with the garlic, olive oil, wine, salt and pepper, push a little of the mixture into the squid sac. Place in a single layer in an ovenproof dish and bake for 15–20 minutes.

Arrange the salad leaves on individual plates, lay the squid on top and spoon over some of the hot juices. Sprinkle with parsley and serve with the remaining juices.

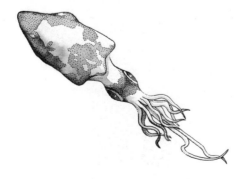

Stir-fried Squid with Fresh
Ginger and Spring Onions

This makes a wonderfully quick supper dish that is ready in minutes. Serve it with egg noodles that take about the same amount of time to cook. Queen scallops or sliced monkfish could replace the squid in this recipe.

SERVES 4

2 tablespoons extra virgin
    olive oil
750 g/1½ lb squid, cleaned
    (page 6) and cut into
    fine rings
125 g/4 oz shelled peas or
    frozen petit pois,
    defrosted

1 bunch of spring onions,
    chopped
1 tablespoon ginger root,
    finely chopped
2 tablespoons dry white
    vermouth
salt and freshly ground
    black pepper

Heat the oil in a frying pan or wok, add the squid and cook over high heat, stirring constantly, for 1–2 minutes.

Toss in the peas, spring onions and ginger, and heat through for 1–2 minutes, still stirring.

Sprinkle on the vermouth and season with salt and pepper. Mix well and serve immediately.

Squid Stuffed with Pea Risotto

Although filling the squid sacs with the risotto is quite fiddly, it is so delicious that it is worth the bother.

SERVES 4

12 × 10 cm/4 in squid

For the risotto:
1 small onion
50 g/2 oz butter
175 g/6 oz arborio rice
500 ml/ 18 fl oz fish or
    chicken stock
125 g/4 oz shelled peas,
    defrosted if frozen
salt and freshly ground
    black pepper

2 tablespoons extra virgin
    olive oil
300 g/10 oz sugar snap or
    mange tout peas, to
    serve

Clean the squid (page 6). Chop the tentacles and set them aside.

Follow the Basic Risotto recipe (page 101) using the above ingredients. Soften the onion in half of the butter. When the rice is almost cooked, melt the remaining butter in a small frying pan and sauté the chopped tentacles for 2 minutes. Add the peas, stir together and add to the risotto. Season with salt and pepper. Allow to cool slightly, then stuff the mixture into the squid sacs using your fingers or a small spoon.**

Heat the oven to 190°C/375°F/Gas Mark 5.

Pour the oil into an ovenproof dish, lay the squid in it and season with salt and pepper. Bake for 15–20 minutes.

Just before the squid is ready, plunge the sugar snap or mange tout peas into boiling salted water for 2 minutes. Drain and arrange on individual plates. Place the squid in the middle and serve.

** *Can be prepared in advance up to this point.*

Swordfish and Mixed Pepper Kebabs

SERVES 6

150 ml/¼ pt extra virgin
    olive oil
juice of 1 lemon
2 tablespoons chopped
    fresh basil or the leaves
    stripped from 3 sprigs of
    thyme
salt and freshly ground
    black pepper
1.5 kg/3 lb swordfish,
    shark or tuna steaks

1 yellow and 1 green
    pepper, grilled, peeled
    (page 5), seeded and cut
    into thick strips
4 tomatoes, skinned, seeded
    and quartered
2 mild red onions, peeled
    and cut into wedges
    (optional)

Mix together the olive oil, lemon juice, herbs, salt and pepper. Cut the fish into good-sized cubes and marinate for 15–20 minutes.

Heat the grill to maximum temperature.

Alternate pieces of pepper, tomato, onion (if you are using it) and fish on the skewers. Grill for 8–10 minutes, turning the kebabs half-way through the cooking time. Serve with some of the marinade poured over the skewers.

Swordfish Steaks with Pesto and Tomato Concassé

SERVES 4

125 ml/4 fl oz dry white
    wine
4 × 150 g/5 oz swordfish
    or tuna steaks, 2 cm/¾ in
    thick
3 tablespoons extra virgin
    olive oil
salt and freshly ground
    black pepper

4 tablespoons Pesto (page
    10)
350 g/12 oz Tomato
    Concassé (page 6)
1 lemon, quartered, to
    serve

Pour the wine into a large heavy-bottomed pan. Brush the swordfish
steaks with olive oil, season with salt and pepper and put them into
the pan. Cover and simmer for 2–3 minutes. Spread 1 tablespoon of
pesto over each steak, cover, and cook for a further 2–3 minutes.
Serve with the tomato concassé and lemon quarters.

Swordfish Steaks with Salsa

Dense textured fish such as swordfish are greatly helped by even a brief spell in a marinade. It provides both flavour and moisture. The salsa provides the bright colours and zip.

SERVES 4

4 × 150 g/5 oz swordfish steaks, about 2 cm/¾ in thick
4 tablespoons extra virgin olive oil
1 clove garlic, finely chopped
1 red and 1 yellow pepper, grilled, peeled (page 5), seeded and finely chopped
½–1 chilli pepper, seeded and chopped
salt and freshly ground black pepper

1 tablespoon capers
1 tablespoon parsley, chopped

For the marinade:
4 tablespoons extra virgin olive oil
60 ml/2 fl oz white wine
1 clove garlic, crushed
1 pinch of tarragon
salt and freshly ground black pepper

Put the swordfish steaks into a shallow dish. Mix the marinade ingredients together and pour them over the top. Leave for 2–3 hours in a cool place, turning them occasionally.**

Heat 3 tablespoons of oil in a small saucepan, add the garlic, peppers and chilli. Stir together for 2 minutes. Season with salt and pepper. Remove from the heat and keep warm.

Heat the grill or ridged cast-iron grill pan to maximum temperature.

Remove the swordfish steaks from the marinade, pat them dry with kitchen paper, then brush them with the remaining tablespoon of oil. Grill the steaks for 4 minutes on each side or 2 minutes in a grill pan.

Add the capers and parsley to the warm peppers and serve with the fish.

** *Can be prepared in advance up to this point.*

Blackened Tuna

Fish seared with a coating of dried herbs and black pepper comes from the Cajun cooking found in New Orleans.

SERVES 4

1 tablespoon coarsely ground black peppercorns	4 × 150g/5oz tuna steaks, 1 cm/½ in thick
1 tablespoon dried thyme	2 tablespoons extra virgin olive oil
1 tablespoon dried basil	4 tablespoon butter
¼ teaspoon cayenne pepper	1 lemon, quartered, to
½ teaspoon salt	serve

Mix together the black pepper, thyme, basil, cayenne and salt. Brush the fish with the olive oil and coat with the spices, pressing them in well. Leave for at least 15 minutes.**

Heat a heavy-bottomed frying pan until hot, add the butter and when it is bubbling sauté the fish until well browned on both sides, about 3–4 minutes per side. Serve immediately with the lemon wedges.

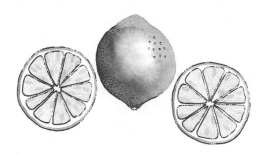

** *Can be prepared in advance up to this point.*

Chopped Tuna Steak with Mixed Pepper Relish

Tuna with its meaty flavour is excellent grilled like a chopped steak. It is simple but tasty and is enhanced by the attractive multi-coloured pepper relish.

SERVES 4

625 g/1 ¼ lb fresh, boned tuna
salt and freshly ground black pepper
1 red pepper, very finely diced
1 green or yellow pepper, very finely diced

1 small red onion, very finely diced
60 ml/2 fl oz extra virgin olive oil, plus extra for frying
1 pinch of chilli powder or cayenne pepper

Cut the tuna into chunks. If possible, use a hand mincer to mince it on a medium/coarse disc. If you do not have a mincer, use the pulse mode of a food processor, but do not over-process.

Season the fish with salt and pepper, and divide the mixture into eight balls, then form them into cakes – a biscuit ring helps to make them neat.

Mix the diced peppers and onion with the olive oil, season, then sprinkle on a small pinch of chilli powder or cayenne pepper. Allow the spiciness to develop before adding any more.**

Wipe a ridged cast-iron grill pan, a griddle pan or a non-stick frying pan with a small amount of olive oil. When it is very hot, cook the cakes for 2–3 minutes on each side.

Arrange on a plain-coloured plate with relish surrounding the cakes.

** *Can be prepared in advance up to this point.*

Tuna Steaks with Caramelized Onions

The fruitiness of caramelized onions needs a well-flavoured fish to balance it and tuna strikes the right note. Serve it with plain boiled potatoes or polenta.

SERVES 6

1 kg/2 lb onions, finely sliced
2 tablespoons extra virgin olive oil
1 tablespoon cider vinegar
2 cloves garlic, chopped
salt and freshly ground black pepper
175 g/6 oz tuna steak per person
1 tablespoon chopped parsley, to serve

Sweat the onions in olive oil in a heavy casserole for 20 minutes, then turn up the heat to caramelize them. Add the vinegar, garlic, salt and pepper and mix well.**

Put the seasoned tuna steaks into the casserole and cover them with the onions. Place the lid on the casserole, turn down the heat, and cook gently for a further 15 minutes. Sprinkle with parsley before serving.

** *Can be prepared in advance up to this point.*

Fillet of Turbot with Tapenade Croûtes

Turbot is a sumptuous fish and wonderful for very special occasions. It bakes beautifully and makes very easy eating on the savoury tapenade-coated croûtes.

SERVES 4

175 g/6 oz turbot or brill
    fillet per person
extra virgin olive oil
salt and freshly ground
    black pepper
4 slices of white bread, with
    crusts removed

4 tablespoons Tapenade
    (page 11)
1 tablespoon finely
    chopped parsley, to
    serve

Brush the turbot fillets with olive oil and season them with salt and pepper. Place in an oiled ovenproof dish and bake for 15 minutes.

While the fish is cooking, fry the slices of bread in a little olive oil until golden. Drain on kitchen paper and keep warm. When the fish is ready, spread the tapenade on the croûtes and place the fish on top. Sprinkle with parsley and serve.

CHICKEN & GAME

Chicken Breasts with Leeks and Celery

This is a very easy and attractive way to serve chicken breasts. A little stuffing goes under the skin to provide flavour and to help keep the breasts moist.

SERVES 6

6 chicken breasts, skin intact
1 tablespoon extra virgin olive oil
40 g/1½ oz butter
2 leeks, finely diced
1 carrot, finely diced
2 sticks celery, finely diced
1 teaspoon fresh chopped tarragon
salt and freshly ground black pepper
1 teaspoon arrowroot
150 ml/¼ pt chicken stock

Pat the breasts dry and trim them into tidy shapes. Push your finger under the skin to detach it on three sides.

Heat the oil with a small knob of butter in a saucepan. Stir in the vegetables, half the tarragon and season. Sauté gently until the vegetables are tender, about 10 minutes. When they have cooled, lift up the skin and spoon a layer of stuffing over the breasts. Place the skin over the stuffing, season and set in a greased shallow baking dish, large enough for the breasts to fit snugly in one layer. Melt the remaining butter and brush it over the skins.**

Heat the oven to 190°C/375°F/Gas Mark 5.

Bake the breasts in the top of the oven for about 25 minutes, or until the meat feels bouncy when touched with a finger. Baste once with the accumulated juices. Remove from the oven and pour the juices into a small saucepan. Mix the arrowroot with the stock and add to the saucepan with the remaining tarragon. Boil for 1 minute to thicken slightly. Serve the breasts with a spoonful of the sauce poured over them.

** *Can be prepared in advance up to this point.*

Chicken Breasts Cooked in Mustard and Yoghurt

Preparation for this dish takes only a few minutes and can be done well in advance – a great standby when your cooking time is limited. Rice or couscous and a salad go well with it.

SERVES 4

4 tablespoons Dijon
  mustard
6 tablespoons Greek-style
  natural yoghurt
2 tablespoons extra virgin
  olive oil
2 cloves garlic, chopped
2 teaspoons cumin
1 teaspoon ground coriander

1 pinch of cayenne pepper
salt and freshly ground
  black pepper
4 skinned free-range
  chicken breasts
1 tablespoon chopped fresh
  coriander, to serve

Mix all the ingredients together, except for the fresh coriander, and smear them over the chicken breasts. Leave them in the marinade for 2–3 hours or longer if convenient, turning occasionally.**

Heat the oven to 190°C/375°F/Gas Mark 5.

Place the chicken in an ovenproof dish and cover with the yoghurt mixture. Bake for 35 minutes. Sprinkle with the chopped coriander and serve.

** *Can be prepared in advance up to this point.*

Garlic Chicken

Garlic is transformed when it is roasted and the large number of cloves in this recipe will impart a subtle flavour to the chicken and not overwhelm it. The cloves become very sweet and soft and are delicious. It is particularly good with the first garlic of the new season.

SERVES 4

1.5–1.75/3½–4 lb free-range chicken
40 cloves unpeeled garlic
1 large bouquet garni
90 ml/3 fl oz extra virgin olive oil

salt and freshly ground black pepper
flour and water for the dough

Choose a heavy casserole that fits the chicken snugly and pack the garlic and bouquet garni around it. Pour the olive oil over the chicken and season with salt and pepper.

Preheat the oven to 180°C/350°F/Gas Mark 4.

Make a firm dough with flour and water and roll it into a long sausage. Press the dough on to the moistened edges of the casserole and pinch the ends together to join them. Cover with the lid and press down firmly.**

Bake for 15 minutes, then turn the oven down to 150°C/300°F/Gas Mark 2. Bake for a further 1½–2 hours depending on the size of the chicken.

Break the dough seal and remove the chicken and garlic. Carve the chicken and serve with the garlic cloves.

** *Can be prepared in advance up to this point.*

Chicken Breasts Stuffed with Wild Mushrooms and Prosciutto

Lacy caul fat is perfect for wrapping around lean cuts of meat to keep them moist while roasting. It can be ordered from good butchers and will either come fresh or, more often, dry-salted. Soak the dry-salted fat in warm water to soften before wrapping it around the meat.

SERVES 4

25 g/1 oz butter
1 leek, diced
1 clove garlic, chopped
150 g/5 oz wild mushrooms, such as porcini or chanterelles
50 g/2 oz prosciutto ham, finely diced
2 tablespoons chopped parsley
1 teaspoon chopped thyme
salt and freshly ground black pepper

1 free-range egg, beaten
4 free-range chicken breasts
1 piece caul fat, 30 × 60 cm/12 × 24 in, cut into quarters
2 red onions, cut into fine rings
125 ml/4 fl oz dry white wine or chicken stock

Melt the butter in a heavy-bottomed pan and soften the leek with the garlic. Wipe the mushrooms with a damp cloth to remove any grit. Chop them finely and add to the pan. Cook gently for 10 minutes until the juices have evaporated. Stir in the prosciutto, parsley and thyme, and season with salt and pepper. Remove from the heat and mix in the egg.

With a rolling pin or cleaver flatten the chicken breasts to an even 1 cm/½ in thickness. Take a very sharp knife and from one side cut open the meat leaving the two edges and the other side joined so that it forms a pocket for the stuffing.

Heat the oven to 190°C/375°F/Gas Mark 5.

Divide the stuffing between the chicken breasts. Wrap each breast in a rectangle of caul fat. Place the onion rings in the bottom of an ovenproof dish with the chicken on top. Pour the wine or stock into the dish and cover with foil.** Bake for 20 minutes, then uncover and return to the oven for 10 minutes to finish cooking. Serve the chicken on the onions with the juices spooned over.

Note: 15 g/ ½ oz dried porcini mushrooms can be used in place of the fresh wild mushrooms. Soak them for 30 minutes in boiling water. Rub off any grit under cold running water. Chop the mushrooms and filter the soaking liquid. Simmer the mushrooms for a few minutes in the strained liquid. Add the mushrooms to the stuffing and use the liquid in place of the wine or stock to pour around the chicken before it bakes.

** *Can be prepared in advance up to this point.*

Roast Chicken with Stuffings

The following three recipes are for roast free-range chicken stuffed under the skin instead of in the body cavity. Look for French chickens from the Landes. They are allowed to roam in acres of ground and their flavour is exceptional.

Prepare the bird the same way for all the stuffings: slip a hand under the skin at the neck end and, taking care not to split it, gently separate it from the flesh.

1.5–1.75 kg/3½–4 lb CHICKEN – SERVES 4

Courgette Stuffing

500 g/1 lb courgettes,
   grated, salted and
   drained for 30 minutes
50 g/2 oz butter
50 g/2 oz grated Parmesan
   or Pecorino cheese

salt and freshly ground
   black pepper
extra virgin olive oil

Wrap the courgettes in a clean tea towel and squeeze out the remaining juices. Heat the butter in a large heavy-bottomed pan, add the courgettes and cook gently until they are soft. Stir in the cheese and season with pepper and a little salt if necessary. Leave to cool.

Gently ease a small handful of the courgette mixture under the loosened skin and over each leg and the remainder over the breast. Brush the chicken with olive oil and season with salt and pepper.**

Heat the oven to 200°C/400°F/Gas Mark 6.

Roast the chicken for 20 minutes, then lower the heat to 180°C/350°F/Gas Mark 4. Continue cooking for a further 40–55 minutes depending on the size of the bird.

** *Can be prepared in advance up to this point.*

Mascarpone Stuffing

125 g/4 oz mascarpone
  cheese
8 large basil leaves, finely
  chopped

salt and freshly ground
  black pepper
extra virgin olive oil

Mix the mascarpone with the basil and season with salt and pepper. Stuff, brush with olive oil, season** and bake as for the previous recipe.

Note: This stuffing is very successful with chicken leg joints. Place a layer of the mascarpone stuffing (you can substitute the basil with other herbs – tarragon or chervil for instance) under the skin, place in a shallow roasting tin, and bake in a moderate oven for about 25 minutes. Good hot or cold.

Mushroom Stuffing

The skin won't break if you're careful. The chicken will bulge but the mushrooms give it a delicious taste.

2 cloves garlic, crushed
3 tablespoons extra virgin
  olive oil
salt and freshly ground
  black pepper

7 large flat field
  mushrooms, 8 cm/3 in
  diameter

Mix the garlic with 2 tablespoons of the olive oil and season with salt and pepper. Brush the mushrooms with the mixture and slide them gently between the skin and the flesh, smooth side upwards: one over each leg, two each side of the breastbone and the remaining one covering the wishbone. Tuck the loose neck skin under the bird and secure with an orange stick. Brush the chicken with the remaining olive oil and season with salt and pepper.** Roast as for the Courgette Stuffing (page 150).

** *Can be prepared in advance up to this point.*

Vegetable Couscous with Chicken Balls

The list of ingredients for this recipe may seem daunting but many are just spices and the finished result will provide an unusual and complete main course. If you omit the chicken it will be a vegetarian feast.

SERVES 4

175 g/6 oz chick peas
4 chicken thighs, boned and skinned
3 tablespoons chopped coriander
salt and freshly ground or cracked black pepper
25 g/1 oz fine fresh breadcrumbs
25 g/1 oz butter
1 onion, chopped
$\frac{1}{4}$ teaspoon turmeric
1 pinch of cayenne pepper
1 pinch of saffron threads
1 cinnamon stick
$\frac{1}{2}$ teaspoon cinnamon
$\frac{1}{2}$ teaspoon ginger
$\frac{1}{2}$ small swede, cut into 1-cm/$\frac{1}{2}$-in cubes
3 medium carrots, cut into 5-cm/2-in sticks

4 small or 2 medium parsnips, quartered and cut into 2.5-cm/1-in pieces
125 g/4 oz ready-to-eat dried apricots, finely sliced
125 g/4 oz raisins
1 teaspoon harissa sauce, plus extra to serve
2 tablespoons chopped parsley
3 tablespoons extra virgin olive oil
500 ml/18 fl oz water
250 g/8 oz couscous
75 g/3 oz pine nuts
150 g/5 oz shelled peas

Soak the chick peas overnight, drain and bring to the boil in a pan of cold water. Drain again, re-cover generously with fresh water and simmer until tender. Add salt when they are nearly tender.

While the chick peas are cooking, place the meat from the chicken thighs in the bowl of a food processor and whiz until thoroughly chopped. Add 1 tablespoon coriander, salt and pepper and process again briefly. Remove form the bowl and mix in the breadcrumbs. Using floured hands, from the mixture into sixteen balls the size of large marbles. Cover and refrigerate.

When the chick peas are cooked, drain them and retain 600 ml/1 pt of the water. Heat the butter in a large heavy-bottomed casserole and soften the onion. Add all the spices and stir well. Season with salt and plenty of pepper.**

Mix the swede, carrots, parsnips, apricots, raisins and chick peas into the casserole and pour in the water from the chick peas. Stir in the harissa with the remaining 2 tablespoons of coriander and the parsley. Season with salt and cover. Simmer for 15 minutes.

While the vegetables are cooking, brown the chicken balls all over in 2 tablespoons of the oil. Bring the salted water to the boil for the couscous. Add the chicken balls to the vegetables and simmer together for a further 10 minutes.

Pour the couscous into the boiling water, turn off the heat and leave for about 5 minutes for the liquid to be absorbed.

Heat the remaining tablespoon of oil in a small pan and toast the pine nuts. Leave to drain on kitchen paper.

Add the peas to the vegetables and heat through. Pour the couscous into a large shallow dish and spoon the chicken balls and vegetables over the top. Sprinkle with pine nuts and serve. Pass some extra harissa around for any guests who enjoy hot food.

** *Can be prepared in advance up to this point.*

Chicken with Pepper and Sun-dried Tomato Sauce

SERVES 4

For the marinade:
60 ml/2 fl oz extra virgin
  olive oil
2 cloves garlic, crushed
2 tablespoons chopped
  marjoram
juice of ½ lemon

1.5–1.75 kg/3½–4 lb free-
  range chicken, jointed
salt and freshly ground
  black pepper
450 ml/¾ pt Red Pepper
  Sauce (page 11)

75 g/3 oz sun-dried
  tomatoes, drained and
  sliced
12 Kalamata olives, stoned
  and chopped

To serve: 1 tablespoon
  chopped parsley or
  chervil
grated rind of 1 well-
  scrubbed or unwaxed
  lemon

Mix the marinade ingredients together in a large bowl, add the chicken pieces and coat them in the mixture. Cover and leave in a cool place for 2–3 hours, turning occasionally.**

Heat the oven to 200°C/400°F/Gas Mark 6.

Remove the chicken from the marinade, season with salt and pepper and place in an ovenproof dish. Cook for 30–35 minutes.

Five minutes before the chicken is ready, warm up the pepper sauce and add the sun-dried tomatoes and olives.

Place the chicken on a serving dish and spoon the pepper sauce over the top. Sprinkle with the parsley or chervil mixed with the lemon rind.

** *Can be prepared in advance up to this point.*

Barbary Duck Breasts in Soy and Sesame Oil

Barbary ducks are far less fatty than the traditional Aylesbury. They are available in most supermarkets and are darker fleshed with a rich, almost gamey, flavour.

SERVES 4

4 Barbary duck breasts	*For the marinade*:
2 large onions, finely sliced	2 tablespoons sesame oil
salt and freshly ground	1 tablespoon soy sauce
black pepper	2 cloves garlic, crushed

Mix together the marinade ingredients. Place the duck breasts in a shallow dish and pour the marinade over the top. Leave in a cool place for at least 2 hours, turning once.**

Heat the oven to 220°C/425°F/Gas Mark 7.

Lay the onions in a thin layer in the bottom of a shallow ovenproof dish and place the duck breasts on top with the marinade. Season with salt and pepper.

Place in the oven for 10 minutes then turn the heat down to 190°C/375°F/Gas Mark 5 for a further 15 minutes. If you prefer the meat to be well done, add 5–10 minutes to the cooking time.

Remove the duck and keep it warm. Quickly caramelize the onions either in a pan on the hob or by turning up the oven temperature. Drain off the fat and arrange the onions on individual plates with the pan juices. Place the duck breasts on top.

** *Can be prepared in advance up to this point.*

Guinea Fowl with Plums

Guinea fowl has excellent flavour but it can be on the dry side. This method of cooking keeps it beautifully moist. The plum sauce, particularly if it is left slightly sharp, complements the birds well.

SERVES 8

2 tablespoons extra virgin
   olive oil
25 g/1 oz butter, plus extra
12 shallots, finely sliced
2 guinea fowl, jointed into
   quarters
150 ml/¼ pt dry white wine
salt and freshly ground
   black pepper

12 large ripe plums
2–3 tablespoons caster
   sugar
2 × 2.5 cm/1 in pieces of
   stem ginger, finely
   chopped
1 tablespoon syrup from
   the ginger

Heat the oven to 160°C/325°F/Gas Mark 3.

Heat the oil and butter in a large heavy-bottomed casserole and sauté the shallots until they are golden. Remove the shallots and brown the seasoned guinea fowl a few pieces at a time. Remove the last pieces from the casserole, pour away any fat and deglaze with the wine. Replace the shallots and joints, arranging them in one overlapping layer. Season with salt and pepper, cover, and simmer in the oven for 25 minutes.

While the casserole is cooking, put eight of the plums into a saucepan in a single layer. Just cover with water and add the sugar. Simmer for 10 minutes or until the flesh is soft. Remove the plums from the pan with a slotted spoon and stone them. Purée the plums in a food processor or blender. Boil the plum cooking syrup until it starts to thicken. Add the plum purée, ginger and ginger syrup.**

Remove the lid from the casserole, turn the heat up to 200°C/400°F/ Gas Mark 6 and bake for a further 10 minutes.

Halve the retained plums and, keeping their shapes, slice them finely. Place a piece of guinea fowl on each plate with a fan of plum slices. Add a knob of butter to the sauce and quickly reheat it. Spoon the sauce around the meat and serve with small well-flavoured potatoes.

** *Can be prepared in advance up to this point.*

Hare in Port and Mulberry Jelly

If you are lucky enough to have a mulberry tree in your garden and make jelly from the fruit, use it in this recipe – if not, redcurrant jelly makes a good alternative.

SERVES 4

50 g/2 oz butter
250 g/8 oz streaky bacon, cut into strips
1 onion, chopped
4 hind leg hare joints
3 tablespoons flour, seasoned with salt and pepper

bouquet garni
300 ml/½ pt game or chicken stock
salt and freshly ground black pepper
125 ml/4 fl oz port
1–2 tablespoons mulberry or redcurrant jelly

Melt the butter in a heavy casserole and soften the bacon and onion. Turn the hare joints in 2 tablespoons of the flour, place in the casserole and brown them with the bacon and onions. Add the bouquet garni and stock. Season with salt and pepper. Simmer gently for 1–1¼ hours until tender.**

Mix together 1 tablespoon of the remaining seasoned flour with the port and jelly and add it to the casserole. Bring it back to the boil and simmer for 5 minutes. Serve with garlic potatoes and a green vegetable.

** *Can be prepared in advance up to this point.*

Grilled Partridge

SERVES 2

2 young partridges, with
   livers if possible
2 tablespoons lemon juice
1 tablespoon honey
2 tablespoons light soy
   sauce

1 teaspoon dried thyme
4 tablespoons butter
175 ml/6 fl oz red wine
salt and freshly ground
   black pepper
2 slices of toast, to serve

Cut the partridges down the back to one side of the centre backbone, then cut away the backbone. Flatten out the birds and marinate for 1 hour in a mixture made from the lemon juice, honey, soy sauce and thyme.**

Heat the grill and when ready grill the partridges for 8 minutes skin side down. Turn them over, smear the breasts with half of the butter and grill for another 8 minutes, or until just cooked. Adjust the distance from the heat if the partridges threaten to burn, but do not overcook them.

Meanwhile, sauté the livers very briefly in the rest of the butter. Deglaze the pan with a splash of wine, add to the livers and mash with salt and pepper.

Serve the partridges on toast spread with the liver paste. Deglaze the grill pan with the remaining wine, boil hard for a few minutes and pour it over the partridges.

** *Can be prepared in advance up to this point.*

Partridge with Lentils

SERVES 4

150 g/5 oz Puy lentils
1 onion, pierced with 2
  cloves
1 carrot, quartered
bouquet garni
2 tablespoons mild red wine
  vinegar
salt and freshly ground
  black pepper
4 young partridges, with
  livers

butter
4 rashers of fat unsmoked
  bacon
2 shallots, finely chopped
1 tablespoon extra virgin
  olive oil
2 tablespoons cognac
5 tablespoons red wine
2 tablespoons finely
  chopped coriander, to
  serve

Pick over the lentils and soak them in cold water for 1 hour. Rinse them and place in a saucepan with the onion, carrot and bouquet garni. Add water to cover, and simmer gently until the lentils are tender, about 1 hour. Drain if necessary and discard the vegetables and bouquet garni. Season with the vinegar, salt and pepper and set aside.**

Preheat the oven to 230°C/450°F/Gas Mark 8.

Wipe the partridges and season. Place a knob of butter in each cavity and wrap each partridge in bacon. Smear a roasting tin with butter and set the partridge breast side down in the tin. Place in the oven and roast for 20 minutes. Turn over half-way through the cooking time.

Meanwhile, sauté the shallots in the oil until soft, add the livers and fry quickly to seal. Deglaze the pan with the cognac, season and set aside.

Place the partridges on a heated serving dish and keep warm. Deglaze the pan with the red wine. Tip the lentils into the pan and heat on top of the cooker. When the lentils are hot, spoon them around the partridges. Quickly heat the livers and spoon them over the lentils. Sprinkle with coriander and serve.

** *Can be prepared in advance up to this point.*

Pot-roasted Partridge with Shallots

Pot-roasting game birds is a successful way of keeping them from drying out. You can also add a variety of vegetables to the pot which will add flavour and can then be served with the game. It is also good for guinea fowl, which tends to be on the dry side.

SERVES 4

2 tablespoons finely chopped parsley	1 tablespoon extra virgin olive oil
100 g/3½ oz butter	16 large shallots, sliced
salt and freshly ground black pepper	4 tablespoons brandy
4 partridges	4 tablespoons port
	150 ml/¼ pt chicken stock

Mix the parsley with 25 g/1 oz of the butter and season with salt and pepper. Place a knob of the parsley mixture inside each bird. Add the oil with 15 g/½ oz of butter in a flameproof casserole and brown the birds on all sides. Remove the birds and discard the fat.

Preheat the oven to 190°C/375°F/Gas Mark 5.

Add 25 g/1 oz of butter to the casserole, followed by the sliced shallots. Stir for a few minutes over gentle heat to soften. Smear the remaining butter over the partridges and place them breast side down on the shallots. Warm the brandy and port in a ladle, set it alight and pour it over the birds. Add the hot stock. Cover snugly with a piece of greaseproof paper and a tight-fitting lid. Place in the oven and roast for 35 minutes.

Remove the partridges to a heated dish, cover loosely with foil and rest for 5 minutes. Divide the shallots among four heated plates, place the partridges on top and serve.

Pigeon Breasts with Balsamic Vinegar Sauce

Wood pigeons are remarkably good value even if only the breasts are used. If you were certain of the age of the bird and knew it to be under four months you would have a delectable squab which would be tender throughout. But supermarket wood pigeons of indeterminate age provide delectable little steaks and the rest of the bird can make a wonderful stock.

SERVES 4

4 wood pigeons
salt and freshly ground
   black pepper
2 tablespoons extra virgin
   olive oil

4 tablespoons balsamic
   vinegar
100 ml/3½ fl oz crème
   fraîche

Remove the breasts from the pigeons by slipping a knife to one side of the breastbone and working it down, keeping it as close to the bone as possible. Place the breasts between two pieces of cling film and flatten slightly with a rolling pin. Season the breasts on both sides with salt and pepper. (Use the carcasses and skin for stock for another dish.)**

Heat the oil in a heavy-bottomed frying pan and when it is very hot seal the breasts quickly on each side, then lower the heat to moderate and give them a further 3 minutes on each side. Press them down with a spatula every now and then. This should give you pink breasts. If they are cooked to a well-done stage they will lose their succulence. Remove the breasts from the pan and keep them warm in a low oven.

Add the balsamic vinegar and boil for 1 or 2 minutes until it is reduced by half. Remove from the heat and stir in the crème fraîche. Serve the pigeon breasts with some of the sauce spooned over them. Mashed potatoes and cabbage would go well with this dish.

** *Can be prepared in advance up to this point.*

Roasted Pigeon Breasts with Sage and Bacon

These roasted pigeon breasts go well with mashed potatoes or a root vegetable purée and any of the brassicas.

SERVES 4

4 pigeons	16 fresh sage leaves
salt and freshly ground	16 thin rashers of
black pepper	unsmoked streaky bacon

Preheat the oven to 230°C/450°F/Gas Mark 8.

Slip a knife to the side of the breastbone, keeping it as close to the bone as possible, and remove the breasts with the top wing joints still attached. Season. Place a sage leaf on each side of each breast and secure by wrapping them in two pieces of bacon.**

Place the breasts in a roasting tin and roast in the top of the oven for 15 minutes. Remove from the oven, cover loosely with foil and leave to rest for 5 minutes before serving.

Poussin Stuffed with Leeks and Pancetta

The stuffing and preparation for the poussin can be prepared completely beforehand. Boning the breasts is not at all difficult and takes very little time. They are not only tasty with their savoury filling but also easy to carve. They go well with grilled polenta or mashed potatoes and all vegetables.

SERVES 6

25 g/1 oz butter, plus extra	65 g/2½ oz fresh brown
2 tablespoons extra virgin	breadcrumbs
olive oil	1 free-range egg, beaten
125 g/4 oz pancetta or	salt and freshly ground
streaky bacon	black pepper
2 leeks, finely chopped	3 poussins
2 cloves garlic, chopped	½ glass of white wine
12 juniper berries, crushed	(optional)
2 tablespoons chopped	
parsley	

** *Can be prepared in advance up to this point.*

Melt the butter and oil in a small frying pan and briefly fry the pancetta. Stir in the leeks, garlic and juniper berries, and cook until the leeks soften. Remove from the heat and stir in the parsley and breadcrumbs. Bind with the egg and season with pepper and just a bit of salt.

Bone the breast of each poussin by first cutting through the backbone. Work with a short flexible knife, using short strokes. Scrape away the flesh from the carcass, easing the skin and flesh back as you go. Cut the flesh from the sabre-shaped bone near the wing. Wiggle the wing to find the ball-and-socket joint and sever it. Do the same with the thigh bone. Cut against the ridge of the breastbone to free the skin, being careful not to pierce it, and remove. Place the poussin skin side down and season the flesh with salt and pepper. Heap the stuffing down the centre and secure in place with orange sticks. Turn the bird over, shape it and tie the legs together with string. Repeat with the other poussins. Place them in an oiled baking pan and brush with butter.**

Heat the oven to 190°C/375°F/Gas Mark 5.

Roast the poussins for 25–30 minutes. Leave to rest for a few minutes before cutting the birds in half. Deglaze the roasting tin with some water or wine and pour the juices over the poussins. Serve at once.

** *Can be prepared in advance up to this point.*

Quails with Grapes

Cooking quails in vine leaves keeps them moist and gently scents the birds. Not surprisingly the flavour goes particularly well with grapes.

SERVES 4

1 shallot, finely chopped
1 tablespoon butter
2 tablespoons extra virgin olive oil
4 chicken livers
3 tablespoons cognac
32 white grapes, Italia if possible, peeled and pipped
1 teaspoon fresh sage leaves, chopped

salt and freshly ground black pepper
8 quails
8 vine leaves
4 slices unsmoked fatty streaky bacon
175 ml/6 fl oz good game or chicken stock
2 teaspoons arrowroot

Sauté the shallot in the butter and 1 tablespoon of the oil, stirring until the shallot softens. Add the livers and fry for a few minutes until they are lightly cooked – still pink on the inside. Scrape into a bowl. Add 1 tablespoon of the cognac to the pan and scrape up any brown bits from the bottom. Pour this over the livers and add several grapes and the sage. Chop the mixture coarsely and season. Dry the quails with kitchen paper and stuff the cavities with the liver mixture.

Pour boiling water over the vine leaves and leave for 15 minutes to soften and remove any brine, then wipe them dry. Wrap a leaf around each bird and cover with half a rasher of bacon. Hold in place with a piece of string.**

Preheat the oven to 190°C/375°F/Gas Mark 5.

Place 1 tablespoon of oil in a roasting pan large enough to hold the quails in one layer. Arrange the quails in the pan and roast for 35 minutes.

Transfer the quails to a heated platter, remove the string, bacon and vine leaves and discard. Keep the quails warm while you make the sauce.

** *Can be prepared in advance up to this point.*

Discard the grease from the pan, add the remaining cognac and the stock and stir to dissolve the pan juices. Strain into a saucepan. Stir the arrowroot with a few tablespoons of the stock to dissolve. Add it to the sauce in the pan along with most of the remaining grapes. Heat just long enough for the sauce to thicken. Taste for seasoning. Serve the birds with a few tablespoons of sauce and several grapes.

Quails in Peppers

In this recipe the diminutive quail is baked in half a pepper. The nest is lined with pancetta – Italian bacon. Unlike English or Danish bacon, it does not fill the frying pan with white liquid but will brown beautifully in a dry pan and render clear fat. It also tastes good. Most Italian grocers carry it.

SERVES 4

2 large red peppers	8 quails
2 large yellow peppers	salt and freshly ground
250 g/8 oz pancetta or thick	black pepper
unsmoked streaky bacon	8 vine leaves
2 tablespoons extra virgin	
olive oil	

Cut the peppers in half horizontally, cutting through the stem and leaving it attached. Carefully remove the seeds without tearing the peppers. Place under a hot grill, skin side up and grill until the peppers are beginning to show brown blotches and become softer. Peel off the charred skin with wet fingers and set the peppers aside.

Fry the pancetta in a frying pan until it browns. Remove with a slotted spoon and drain on kitchen paper. Pour away all but 1 tablespoon of the fat from the pan, add the olive oil and brown the quails. Season with salt and pepper.

Arrange some pancetta pieces in each pepper half, place the quails on top and scatter over the remaining pancetta.

Put the vine leaves in a bowl and pour boiling water over them. Leave for 10 minutes, then drain. Tuck a leaf over each quail and place in an oiled roasting tin.**

Preheat the oven to 190 °C/375 °F/Gas Mark 5. Roast the quails for 40 minutes. Remove the vine leaves before serving.

** *Can be prepared in advance up to this point.*

Quail Stuffed with Prunes

As this recipe can be prepared in advance right up to the roasting, it makes an impressive dinner party main course. The prepared polenta squares can be grilled swiftly at the last moment (fried bread could be used instead) and the quails placed on them straight from the oven.

SERVES 6

275 g/9 oz pitted prunes
125 ml/4 fl oz medium
    sherry or ruby port
Polenta (page 22), cut into
    12 × 8-cm/3-in squares
3 shallots, chopped
2 cloves garlic, chopped
15 g/½ oz butter
65 g/2½ oz oyster
    mushrooms, chopped

salt and freshly ground
    black pepper
1 tablespoon chopped
    coriander
12 quails
12 rashers streaky bacon
extra virgin olive oil

Soak the prunes overnight in the sherry.

Make the polenta, cut it into squares and set aside.

Soften the shallots and garlic in the butter and add the mushrooms. Cook together gently for 2 minutes and season with salt and pepper. Chop the prunes (which should have completely absorbed the alchohol) and mix them with the shallots and mushrooms. Stir in the coriander and leave to cool.

Wash and dry the quails and stuff the body cavities with the prune mixture. Tie or spear the legs together with an orange stick. Season with salt and a little pepper. Cut the bacon rashers into halves and cover the breasts with them. Arrange the quails on a roasting tray.**

Heat the oven to 190°C/375°F/Gas Mark 5. Roast the quails for 35–40 minutes.

Brush the polenta with olive oil and grill on a very hot ridged cast-iron grill pan or under a grill. Serve the quails on the polenta with a green salad.

** *Can be prepared in advance up to this point.*

Rabbit with Prunes

Fruit eaten with meat is a very English tradition that is apt to horrify the French. They do make an exception though when it comes to prunes – this recipe, using Pruneaux d'Agen, is often found on menus in south-western France. The rabbit needs to be marinated overnight, so start preparation the day before serving.

SERVES 4

1 rabbit, cut into 8
   pieces
175 g/6 oz prunes – not
   the ready-to-eat kind
1 tablespoon extra virgin
   olive oil
15 g/½ oz butter
15 g/½ oz flour
250 g/8 fl oz white wine
300 ml/½ pt chicken stock
1 clove garlic, crushed
salt and freshly ground
   black pepper

1 tablespoon chopped
   parsley, to serve

For the marinade:
150ml/¼ pt white wine
1 large bouquet garni
1 onion, chopped
1 carrot, chopped
6 black peppercorns,
   crushed
1 tablespoon extra virgin
   olive oil

Mix all the marinade ingredients together in a bowl and put in the rabbit pieces, cover and leave overnight in the fridge, turning occasionally.

Pour boiling water over the prunes and leave them to soak for 6 hours.

Take the rabbit joints out of the marinade and dry them on kitchen paper. Heat the oil and butter in a large casserole and brown the pieces all over.

Remove the rabbit from the casserole. Using a slotted spoon, take the onion and carrot out of the marinade and sauté them until they are soft. Sprinkle with the flour and stir until it browns. Stir in the marinade liquid and the white wine. Bring it to the boil and add the stock, garlic and bouquet garni from the marinade. Season with salt and pepper.

Return the rabbit to the casserole, cover, and simmer for 25 minutes. Remove the joints, strain the sauce and pour it back into the casserole. Mash the vegetables into a smooth purée and use it to thicken the liquid slightly. Replace the rabbit and add the drained prunes.** Simmer for 15 minutes until tender.

Transfer the rabbit and prunes to a serving dish and keep them warm. Reduce the sauce until it becomes creamy. Check the seasoning. Pour the sauce over the dish and sprinkle with the parsley.

** *Can be prepared in advance up to this point.*

Rabbit Roasted in Mustard and Breadcrumbs

Be generous with the Dijon mustard – it is really quite mild and is transformed when roasted into a wonderful crispy crust.

SERVES 4

50 g/2 oz butter
salt and freshly ground
   black pepper
1 rabbit, cut into 8 pieces
8 tablespoons Dijon
   mustard
75 g/3 oz fresh
   breadcrumbs

To serve:
125 g/4 oz streaky bacon,
   cut into thin strips
1 tablespoon chopped
   parsley

Heat the butter in a large heavy-bottomed pan and brown the seasoned rabbit joints. Leave to cool.

Heat the oven to 200°C/400°F/Gas Mark 6.

Brush the rabbit pieces with the mustard and roll them in the breadcrumbs. Lay them in a buttered ovenproof dish and bake for 30–35 minutes.

While the rabbit is cooking, crisp the bacon in a pan or under the grill, drain on kitchen paper and keep it warm.

Place the rabbit in a serving dish, scatter the bacon and parsley over the top and serve.

SALADS

Mixed Beans and Peppers Salad

This is a colourful salad that will enliven any meal. Assemble it as late as possible so the black beans do not bleed into the paler ones.

SERVES 6

125 g/4 oz pinto beans
125 g/4 oz white haricot beans
125 g/4 oz black beans
175–250 ml/6–8 fl oz Vinaigrette with added mixed herbs (page 16)
2 shallots, chopped

1 red pepper, seeded and diced
1 yellow or green pepper, seeded and diced
2 tablespoons chopped parsley
salt and freshly ground black pepper

Put the beans into separate bowls and soak them overnight in water. Drain and place them in three pans. Cover with water and bring them to the boil. Drain and re-cover generously with fresh water. Simmer for 40–60 minutes until the beans are cooked. Add salt towards the end of the cooking time and take care not to let them disintegrate. Drain and cool the beans slightly before tossing them separately in the vinaigrette.** Add them to a salad bowl with the shallots, peppers and parsley, and season with salt and pepper. Do not refrigerate before serving.

** *Can be prepared in advance up to this point.*

Chick Pea Salads

These salads are suitable for serving with grilled meats or with other salads for light meals.

SERVES 4

For the following three recipes:

275 g/9 oz chick peas   salt

Rinse and soak the chick peas overnight in water to cover. Rinse the chick peas and bring them to the boil in fresh water, drain and re-cover with cold water. Simmer for 1–2 hours depending on the freshness of the peas. Add salt towards the end of the cooking time when the peas are becoming soft. Remove from the heat when they are floury inside but before they begin to disintegrate.

Chick Pea Salad with Bacon and Peppers

1 medium onion, chopped
3 tablespoons extra virgin
    olive oil
2 garlic cloves, chopped
250 g/8 oz streaky bacon,
    cut into fine strips
2 red peppers, grilled,
    peeled (page 5), seeded
    and sliced into thin strips

salt and freshly ground
    black pepper
2 tablespoons chopped
    parsley, to serve

Sauté the onion in the oil until soft, then add the garlic and bacon. Continue cooking until the fat renders and the onions are golden. Stir in the peppers and season with salt and pepper. Remove from the heat and mix into the cooked chick peas. Scatter with the parsley and serve warm.

Chick Pea Salad with Spring Onions and Parsley

125 ml/4 fl oz extra virgin
  olive oil
grated rind of 1 unwaxed
  or well-scrubbed lemon
juice of ½ lemon
1 bunch of spring onions,
  chopped into small
  pieces

4 tablespoons chopped
  parsley
salt and freshly ground
  black pepper

Cook the chick peas as before. Drain them and while they are still warm, pour the olive oil over them and mix well. Add the remaining ingredients and season with salt and pepper. Serve warm or cold.

Chick Pea Salad with Tomato and Garlic

1 medium onion, chopped
4 tablespoons extra virgin
  olive oil
250 g/8 oz tomatoes,
  skinned, seeded and
  chopped
125 g/4 oz sun-dried
  tomatoes, drained and
  sliced
3 cloves garlic, chopped
1 tablespoon chopped
  mixed herbs, such as
  basil, marjoram and
  parsley

salt and freshly ground
  black pepper

To serve:
1 tablespoon chopped
  parsley
rind from 1 unwaxed or
  well-scrubbed lemon

Sauté the onion in the oil until golden then add the tomatoes, sun-dried tomatoes, garlic and herbs. Season with salt and pepper. Cook together for 5 minutes until the liquid has evaporated.

Pour the mixture over the cooked chick peas and scatter with the parsley and lemon zest.** Serve hot or cold.

** *Can be prepared in advance up to this point.*

Puy Lentil, Red Onion and Feta Salad

The slate-green lentil from Le Puy in the south-west of France has a rich spiciness that makes it the most delicious lentil of all.

SERVES 4

350 g/12 oz Puy lentils
1 medium onion, cut into
    quarters
1 clove garlic, peeled
1 bay leaf
4 tablespoons extra virgin
    olive oil
salt and freshly ground
    black pepper

1 medium red onion,
    quartered, then finely
    sliced
250 g/8 oz Feta cheese,
    crumbled
1 tablespoon chopped
    coriander
Garlic Vinaigrette, made
    with lemon juice (page 16)

Wash and pick over the lentils. Cover with cold water and add the onion, garlic and bay leaf. Simmer for 20–30 minutes until they are soft but not mushy.

Drain the lentils and discard the vegetables. While they are still warm toss the lentils in the olive oil and season with salt and pepper. Leave to cool.**

Just before serving mix all the remaining ingredients into the lentils and dress with the garlic and lemon vinaigrette.

** Can be prepared in advance up to this point.

Pasta Salad with Peas and Prawns

It is best to make a pasta salad only a few hours before you intend to serve it – just long enough for the pasta to cool down. If it is made too far in advance the pasta absorbs the dressing and tends to be on the heavy side.

SERVES 4

350 g/12 oz pasta shells or twists
8 tablespoons extra virgin olive oil
2 small leeks, finely sliced
250 g/8 oz shelled peas, fresh or frozen
250 g/8 oz peeled prawns
1–2 tablespoons lemon juice
1 tablespoon chopped chervil
salt and freshly ground black pepper

Cook the pasta in a large quantity of salted water until *al dente* – firm to the bite. Drain and toss the pasta in 4 tablespoons of olive oil while it is still warm and leave it to cool.**

Using a large heavy-bottomed frying pan, wilt the leeks in 2 tablespoons of olive oil. Stir in the peas and warm them through. Remove from the heat.

Mix all the remaining ingredients together and add them to the leeks and peas. Season with salt and pepper and toss with the pasta.

** *Can be prepared in advance up to this point.*

Pasta Salad with Peppers, Anchovies and Sun-dried Tomatoes

SERVES 4

350 g/12 oz pasta shells or twists

8 tablespoons extra virgin olive oil

2 red peppers, grilled, peeled (page 5), seeded and cut into thin strips

1 tin of anchovies, drained then cut into small pieces

50 g/2 oz sun-dried tomatoes, chopped

50 g/2 oz black olives, stoned and chopped

2 tablespoons chopped chervil

2 tablespoons balsamic vinegar

salt and freshly ground black pepper

Cook the pasta in a large quantity of boiling salted water until *al dente* – firm to the bite. Drain, then toss with 4 tablespoons of the olive oil. Leave to cool.**

Mix all the remaining ingredients together in a large bowl and season with salt and pepper. Add the pasta and toss well.

** *Can be prepared in advance up to this point.*

Pasta Salad with Smoked Salmon and Fennel

Smoked salmon makes delicious pasta salad and is a very good way of using the less expensive smoked salmon pieces. Colonna Granverde is a wonderfully fragrant lemon olive oil. If possible, use it for this recipe.

SERVES 4

350 g/12 oz pasta shells or twists
6–8 tablespoons lemon-flavoured or extra virgin olive oil
1 fennel bulb with feathery greens
lemon juice
salt and freshly ground black pepper
250 g/8 oz smoked salmon pieces, finely sliced

Cook the pasta in a large quantity of boiling, salted water and drain. Toss with half the olive oil and leave to cool.

Cut off the feathery leaves of the fennel, chop and set aside. Peel away any coarse outer stalks of fennel, then finely dice all the stalks. Toss the pasta in a large bowl with the diced fennel and half of the leaves. Pour on the remaining lemon olive oil. Add 1 tablespoon of lemon juice if you have used lemon olive oil, or 3 tablespoons if you are using plain olive oil. Mix well and season with salt and pepper.**

Before serving gently mix in the smoked salmon strips and sprinkle the remaining fennel leaves over the top.

** *Can be prepared in advance up to this point.*

Pasta Salad with Tuna and Capers

SERVES 4

350 g/12 oz pasta twists or shells

8 tablespoons extra virgin olive oil

250 g/8 oz fresh tuna steak

salt and freshly ground black pepper

1 clove garlic, chopped

6–8 spring onions, chopped

2 tablespoons capers

2 tablespoons chopped parsley

1 tablespoon lemon juice

Cook the pasta in a large quantity of boiling salted water. Drain and toss with half the olive oil.

Heat the grill or ridged cast-iron grill pan to maximum temperature. Brush the tuna with a little of the oil and season with salt and pepper. Grill for 3–4 minutes on each side. Leave to cool, then flake with a fork.**

Mix all the other ingredients with the tuna in a large bowl, season, then toss with the pasta.

** Can be prepared in advance up to this point.

Roasted Potato and Fennel Salad

This potato salad is made with roasted potatoes instead of the usual boiled ones. They are tossed with thin strips of fennel, olives and seasoning while still hot. The salad is delicious eaten warm or cold, and is very good with chicken or cold meats.

SERVES 6

750 g/1½ lb new or waxy potatoes such as Charlotte, Nicola, Pink Fir Apple or La Ratte
8 shallots, peeled and quartered
2 teaspoons dried thyme
175 ml/6 fl oz extra virgin olive oil

salt and freshly ground black pepper
1 fennel bulb, trimmed then thinly sliced
12 Kalamata olives, stoned and chopped
3 tablespoons lemon juice

Heat the oven to 200°C/400°F/Gas Mark 6.

Scrub the potatoes and cut them into 2.5 cm/1 in chunks. Place in a baking tin large enough to hold them in one layer. Add the shallots, thyme and 125 ml/4 fl oz of the olive oil. Season with salt and pepper and mix together well. Cover with foil and bake for 15 minutes. Uncover, turn the potatoes and bake for another 20 minutes or until they are just cooked through.

Pour the potatoes and the oily juices into a serving bowl. Add the fennel, olives, remaining oil and lemon juice. Season and toss gently but well. Serve warm or at room temperature.

VEGETABLES

Aubergine Gratin

Most of today's aubergines do not need to have an initial salting. As long as you cut them just before cooking they tend not to be bitter.

SERVES 4

750 g/1½ lb aubergines, sliced into 1 cm/½ in rounds

4 tablespoons extra virgin olive oil

600 ml/1 pt Tomato Sauce (page 12)

1 tablespoon chopped basil

125 g/4 oz Cheddar cheese, grated

salt and freshly ground black pepper

Heat the grill or ridged cast-iron grill pan to maximum temperature.

Brush the aubergine slices with the oil and grill both sides until they are brown.

Heat the oven to 200°C/400°F/Gas Mark 6.

Pour half of the tomato sauce into an ovenproof dish and lay the aubergine slices on top. Mix the basil with the cheese and sprinkle half over the aubergines. Season with salt and pepper. Spoon the remaining tomato sauce on top followed by the rest of the cheese and basil.**

Bake for 20–30 minutes until bubbling and golden.

** *Can be prepared in advance up to this point.*

Broccoli with Peppers and Spring Onions

Broccoli is delicious and looks attractive dressed with olive oil and contrasted with diced red pepper.

SERVES 4

1 red pepper, grilled,
  peeled (page 5), seeded
  and finely sliced
1 clove garlic, chopped
6 spring onions, finely
  chopped
1 tablespoon chopped
  parsley

4 tablespoons extra virgin
  olive oil
1 head broccoli, broken
  into florets
salt and freshly ground
  black pepper

Mix the pepper, garlic, onions and parsley into the oil.

Boil some salted water in a large pan, drop in the broccoli florets and cook for 1 minute, drain and toss them in the oil and pepper mixture.

Season with salt and pepper and serve.

Brussels Sprouts with Walnuts

Sprouts are a winter vegetable, best after the frosts – keep them to serve with winter dishes such as game.

SERVES 4

750 g/1 ½ lb Brussels sprouts
75 g/3 oz butter
125 g/4 oz walnuts,
  chopped

salt and freshly ground
  black pepper

Slice the sprouts finely either using a food processor or by hand.

Melt the butter in a large pan, mix in the sprouts and sauté gently until they are nearly cooked but still crisp. Stir in the walnuts.

Season with salt and pepper and serve.

Nutmeg Cabbage

SERVES 4

1 cabbage – Savoy or other   ½ freshly grated nutmeg
   crisp variety   2 tablespoons wine vinegar
50 g/2 oz butter   150 ml/¼ pt single cream
salt and freshly ground
   black pepper

Remove and discard the outer leaves from the cabbage. Cut the cabbage into quarters. Slice each quarter into three pieces and discard the stem. Shred very finely either by hand or with a food processor.

Melt the butter in a large heavy-bottomed frying pan and toss in the cabbage. Season with salt and pepper and grate in the nutmeg. Add the vinegar and mix thoroughly, cover and leave over a low heat for 2–3 minutes until the cabbage has wilted. Pour in the cream and heat through but do not allow it to boil. Check the seasonings and serve hot with meat, game or good chunky butcher's sausages.

Red Cabbage with Apples

This is one of the few instances when a vegetable dish actually improves by being cooked the day before and reheated. A real winter recipe, it is good with all game and duck.

SERVES 6

2 tablespoons extra virgin   2 tablespoons cider vinegar
   olive oil   salt and freshly ground
1 large onion, finely sliced   black pepper
2 tablespoons caster sugar   ½ grated nutmeg
1 red cabbage, cut into   300 ml/½ pt chicken stock
   quarters and finely   125 ml/4 fl oz yoghurt
   sliced   1 tablespoon flour
2 large cooking apples,
   peeled, cored and sliced

Heat the oil in a large casserole and soften the onion. Sprinkle with the sugar and stir until golden. Mix in the cabbage followed by the apples and vinegar. Season with salt and pepper and the grated nutmeg. Pour in the stock. Cover the pan and simmer very gently for 2–3 hours.**

If you have prepared the cabbage in advance, gently reheat it for 45 minutes. Mix the yoghurt into the flour and stir it into the cabbage. Heat through for 5 minutes before serving.

Carrots with Apricots and Almonds

These carrots are not only perfect served with game – the sweetness complements the rich meat – but they also look wonderful.

SERVES 4

500g/1 lb carrots, sliced finely into rounds
25 g/1 oz butter
2 tablespoons orange juice
1–2 teaspoons sugar
1 teaspoon cinnamon
salt and freshly ground black pepper
50 g/2 oz almond flakes
1 teaspoon extra virgin olive oil
125 g/4 oz ready-to-eat dried apricots, finely sliced

Parboil the carrots in salted water and drain them while they are still a little crisp. Toss the carrots in the butter and add the orange juice, sugar and cinnamon. Return the pan to a low heat and glaze the carrots. Season with salt and pepper.

Sauté the almond flakes until golden brown in the olive oil and drain them on kitchen paper. Mix the apricots in with the carrots and heat through. Scatter with the almonds before serving.

** *Can be prepared in advance up to this point.*

Romano Cauliflower with Sun-dried Tomato and Mustard Sauce

Romano cauliflowers have a nuttier taste than the white variety as well as having beautifully formed green florets. Keep an eye out for them in greengrocers and supermarkets.

SERVES 4

50 g/2 oz butter, softened
2 tablespoons Dijon
   mustard
2 shallots, finely diced
1 cloves garlic, crushed
2 tablespoons chopped
   parsley
75 g/3 oz sun-dried
   tomatoes, chopped

1 Romano cauliflower,
   broken into florets
salt and freshly ground
   black pepper
4 thin strips scrubbed
   lemon peel, finely
   chopped, to serve

Mix the butter and mustard together until smooth, then add the shallots, garlic, parsley and sun-dried tomatoes.

Boil some salted water in a large pan, drop in the cauliflower florets and cook for 1–2 minutes, drain and toss them in the butter mixture.

Season with salt and pepper and pour into a serving dish. Sprinkle with the lemon peel and serve.

Braised Chicory

One of the pleasures of going to French markets during winter is seeing the beautifully arranged piles of pearly white chicory. This method of cooking it has a French influence. It is one of the easiest – no need to parboil first.

SERVES 4

50 g/2 oz butter
750 g/1½ lb chicory,
    trimmed and cut in half
    lengthwise
1 tablespoon lemon juice
1 heaped teaspoon caster
    sugar

salt and freshly ground
    black pepper
1 tablespoon chopped
    parsley, to serve

Heat the oven to 180°C/350°F/Gas Mark 4.

Spread half of the butter over the bottom of an ovenproof dish and lay the chicory on top in a single layer. Sprinkle with lemon juice, sugar, salt and pepper. Dot the remaining butter on top. Cover with foil and bake for 45 minutes.

Remove the foil and replace in the oven for a further 10 minutes. Sprinkle with parsley before serving.

Courgettes Baked with Rice

This is not only a delicious dish but a useful one as it combines a starch with a vegetable. It is good with most fish or fowl.

SERVES 6

1.1 kg/2½ lb firm courgettes
75 g/3 oz long-grained rice
   (not the precooked kind)
3 tablespoons extra virgin
   olive oil
1 large onion, finely
   chopped
2 cloves garlic, finely
   chopped
1 tablespoon flour

500 ml/18 fl oz courgette
   juices plus milk
1 egg, lightly beaten
3 tablespoons finely
   chopped coriander
65 g/2½ oz freshly grated
   Parmesan cheese
salt and freshly ground
   black pepper

Wash and trim the ends off the courgettes before coarsely grating them into a colander set over a bowl. Mix with 2 teaspoons of salt and leave while you prepare the onions and rice.

Boil the rice in a large quantity of salted water for 5 minutes, then drain and set aside.

In a large frying pan heat the oil and sauté the onions and the garlic until translucent, about 8 minutes.

Working over a bowl, take handfuls of the courgettes and squeeze out the liquid. Place the squeezed courgettes in the frying pan with the onion. Cook, stirring, for about 5 minutes then stir in the flour. Measure the courgette juices and add milk to make up the correct amount. Stir this into the the onions and bring to a simmer. Remove from the heat, and add the rice, egg, coriander and all but 2 tablespoons of the cheese. Season before pouring into a greased 30 cm/12 in gratin dish.**

Preheat the oven to 190° C/375°F/Gas Mark 5.

Sprinkle the remaining cheese over the top and bake for 45 minutes.

VARIATION:
Add 250 g/8 oz of chopped sautéed mushrooms when you add the rice, and one extra egg.

** *Can be prepared in advance up to this point.*

Braised Fennel

SERVES 4

4 fennel heads
50 g/2 oz butter
1 tablespoon chopped
    parsley

salt and freshly ground
    black pepper

Trim the fennel and retain the feathery leaves. Blanch the trimmed fennel in salted water for 15 minutes, then plunge them into cold water for 2 minutes. Drain and cut the bulbs into quarters, and shake out any remaining water. Meanwhile, finely chop a tablespoon or two of the fennel leaves and set aside.

Heat the butter in a heavy-bottomed frying pan and braise the fennel until it is golden, sprinkle with the parsley and season with salt and pepper. Remove from the heat.

Place in a serving dish and sprinkle with the fennel leaves.

Leeks with Oyster Mushrooms

SERVES 4

500 g/1 lb leeks, finely
    sliced
50 g/2 oz butter
salt and freshly ground
    black pepper
250 g/8 oz oyster
    mushrooms, finely sliced

2 tablespoons extra virgin
    olive oil
1 clove garlic, chopped
150 ml/¼ pt double cream
1 tablespoon chopped
    chives, to serve

Wilt the leeks in the butter and season with salt and pepper. At the same time, in another pan, sauté the mushrooms in the olive oil with the garlic.

Remove the leeks from the heat and stir in the juices from the mushrooms and then the cream and heat through. Check the seasoning and add the mushrooms.

Pour into a serving dish and scatter the chives over the top.

Lentil Purée with Crème Fraîche

SERVES 4

250 g/8 oz Puy lentils
1 onion, cut into quarters
1 clove garlic, peeled
1 bay leaf

salt and freshly ground
    black pepper
3 tablespoons crème fraîche

Wash and pick over the lentils. Turn into a large pan, cover with water and add the onion, garlic and bay leaf. Simmer for 30–40 minutes, until the lentils begin to disintegrate. Remove from the heat, drain, and pick out the onion, garlic and bay leaf. Season with salt and pepper and stir in the crème fraîche. Serve hot.

Baked Shredded Parsnips

This wonderfully simple dish can be popped into the oven at the same time as a roast – try it with the quail recipe (page 167) instead of the polenta.

SERVES 4

1 kg/2 lb parsnips
125 g/4 oz butter, cut into
    cubes

salt and freshly ground
    pepper

Finely grate the peeled parsnips either in a food processor or by hand.

Heat the oven to 200°C/400°F/Gas Mark 6.

Butter a shallow ovenproof dish and make a layer of half of the parsnips, dot it with half of the butter and season with salt and pepper. Cover with the remaining parsnips and butter and season again.

Bake in the oven for 45–55 minutes until golden, checking regularly that the top is not burning. Cover with foil if it looks as if the parsnips will become too dark and then uncover the dish for the last 5 minutes.

Potatoes with Garlic and Cream

A very simple way of making mashed potatoes a bit more interesting.

SERVES 4

750 g/1 ½ lb floury potatoes,   salt and freshly ground
  peeled   black pepper
4 cloves garlic, peeled   90–125 ml/3–4 fl oz single
freshly ground nutmeg   cream

Place the potatoes and the garlic cloves in a pan and cover with water. Add salt and bring to the boil. Simmer until the potatoes are cooked. Drain, retaining the cooking water. Mash the potatoes and the garlic together and add as much of the cooking water as necessary to make a firm purée. Season with nutmeg, salt and pepper and add the cream a little at a time so that it does not become too runny.

Roast Shallots

This is a good vegetable dish to serve with game.

SERVES 4

24 shallots   salt and freshly ground
3 tablespoons extra virgin   black pepper
  olive oil

Peel the shallots. Cut two horizontal slices three-quarters of the way down the shallots, keeping them intact at the root end. Place them in a bowl and toss with the olive oil. Season with salt and pepper.

Heat the oven to 190°C/375°F/Gas Mark 5.

Lay the shallots on a roasting tray or dish and cook for 30–40 minutes until they are brown and the segments have opened up.

Spinach with Bacon and Pine Nuts

SERVES 4

50 g/2 oz pine nuts
1 tablespoon extra virgin
   olive oil
1 kg/2 lb spinach, washed
   and stalks removed
25 g/1 oz butter

8 rashers streaky bacon, cut
   into 1 cm/½ in strips
2 cloves garlic, crushed
salt and freshly ground
   black pepper

Roast the pine nuts in the olive oil until golden, then leave to drain on kitchen paper.

Place the wet spinach in a large pan over a low heat, cover and leave to wilt. Remove from the heat and drain. Press out as much of the moisture as possible and chop roughly.

Heat the butter in a large heavy-bottomed pan and crisp the bacon with the garlic. Add the spinach, season with salt and pepper, heat through and scatter with the roasted pine nuts.

Spinach with Sesame Seeds

SERVES 4

1 kg/2 lb spinach, washed
   and stalks removed
2 tablespoons extra virgin
   olive oil
2 tablespoons sesame seeds

1 tablespoon caster sugar
1 tablespoon soy sauce
salt and freshly ground
   black pepper

Place the wet spinach in a large pan over a low heat, cover and leave to wilt. Remove from the heat and drain. Press out as much of the moisture as possible and chop roughly.

Heat the oil in a large heavy-bottomed pan and roast the sesame seeds until they are golden. Add the spinach and heat it through. Combine the sugar with the soy sauce and sprinkle it on the spinach. Mix well and season with salt and pepper.

Baked Squash with Herb Butter

There is now a large selection of home-grown and imported squash to choose from. They are a very versatile vegetable and can be baked, roasted, puréed or stuffed. The flavour and texture varies from bland and watery to the deliciously firm and nutty varieties used here.

SERVES 4

1 large or 2 small butternut squash *or* 2 acorn squash
salt and freshly ground black pepper

75 g/3 oz Herb Butter (page 13) using a mixture of fresh herbs

Heat the oven to 200°C/400°F/Gas Mark 6.

Halve the squash, scoop out the seeds and season with salt and pepper. Place a spoonful of the herb butter in each hollow. Bake in an ovenproof dish until the flesh is tender, about 50–70 minutes depending on the size of the squash.

After 40 minutes, remove them from the oven and prod the flesh all over with a fork to allow the butter to seep in. Take care not to puncture the outer skin. Replace in the oven to finish cooking. Cut the large butternut in half again before serving.

PUDDINGS

Apple and Almond Cream Tart

Almond cream is an excellent base for other fruit tarts. Try it with pears, nectarines, peaches or apricots.

SERVES 6–8

Sweet Shortcrust Pastry (page 20)	125 g/4 oz ground almonds
125 g/4 oz caster sugar	1 tablespoon cream
125 g/4 oz butter	5 large Cox apples, peeled, cored and halved
1 egg	4 tablespoons apricot jam
1 egg yolk	1 tablespoon lemon juice
1 tablespoon plain flour	

Roll out and line a 25-cm/10-in tin with the pastry. Chill until firm. Place a baking sheet in oven and heat to 200°C/400°F/Gas Mark 6.

Whisk the sugar and butter together until the mixture becomes pale. Mix in the egg, egg yolk, flour, ground almonds and cream. Pour the mixture into the pastry case and spread it out evenly.

Slice the apples crosswise keeping the slices together. Arrange nine of the halves, rounded side upwards, on the pastry cream, like the spokes of a wheel. Use the tenth for the space in the centre. Press the fruit firmly into the cream and brush with half of the jam.

Bake for 15 minutes; turn the oven down to 150°C/300°F/Gas Mark 2, and bake for a further 20 minutes.

While the tart is in the oven, melt the remaining jam with the lemon juice and leave to cool until it begins to thicken.

When the tart has risen and browned, paint the top with the jam and lemon juice, and return it to the oven for a further 5 minutes. Remove from the oven, leave to stand for 10 minutes or while you are eating your main course. Serve warm.

Kumquat Tart

A refreshing slim tart made from candied kumquats. The kumquats are set on a crisp sweet pastry base and baked in a light creamy custard.

SERVES 10–12

Sweet Shortcrust Pastry
   (page 20)

For the kumquats:
500 g/1 lb kumquats
225 g/7½ oz caster sugar
150 ml/¼ pt water

For the cream:
1 egg
1 egg yolk
200 ml/7 fl oz whipping
   cream
2 tablespoons Cointreau
   or other orange liqueur

Roll out and line a shallow 25 cm/10 in tart tin. Refrigerate for 15 minutes.

Preheat the oven to 190°C/375°F/Gas Mark 5 and bake the pastry blind (page 19). Reduce the oven temperature to 180°C/350°F/Gas Mark 4 and place a baking sheet in the centre.

Meanwhile, wash and dry the kumquats. Cut them in half lengthwise and remove any pips. Place in a medium-sized saucepan with the sugar and water. Simmer together for about 25 minutes, or until the kumquats look glazed and the syrup is thick. Using a slotted spoon, scoop out the kumquats and place in the tart. Arrange them cut side down in an even layer. Spoon over the remaining syrup from the pan, heating it with a little water if necessary. Whisk the egg, egg yolk, cream and liqueur together. Pour over the kumquats and bake for 15 minutes, or until the custard is set and golden.** Serve at room temperature.

** *Can be prepared in advance up to this point.*

Lemon Tart

A luscious and irresistible lemon tart that is also simple to prepare.

SERVES 8

Sweet Shortcrust Pastry
  (page 20)
9 free-range eggs
400 g/14 oz caster sugar
250 ml/8 fl oz lemon juice
  – about 5 lemons

grated rind of 3 unwaxed
  or well-scrubbed lemons
250 ml/8 fl oz double or
  whipping cream
icing sugar

Roll out and line a 25 × 4 cm/10 × 1½ in tart tin with a removable base. Chill until firm.

Place a baking sheet in the oven and preheat the oven to 190°C/ 375°F/Gas Mark 5. Bake the pastry blind (page 19).

Whisk together the eggs and sugar until the sugar has melted and the mixture is pale yellow. Still whisking, mix in the lemon juice and zest followed by the cream. Leave for 5 minutes then skim off the bubbles.

Pour three-quarters of the mixture into the warm pastry case and place in the oven before carefully spooning in the rest. Bake for 25–30 minutes, until the lemon is set. Leave to cool.** Remove from the tin and cover with a light sprinkling of icing sugar just before serving.

** *Can be prepared in advance up to this point.*

Caramelized Upside-down Pear Tart

You may recognize this as a close relation of the famous *Tarte des Demoiselles Tatin*. It justly has become a classic and this pear version is every bit as good as the apple one. The secret for a luscious caramelized topping is in cooking the pears on top of the stove before baking the tart in the oven.

SERVES 8–10

2 kg/4½ lb firm but ripe
    pears, such as Anjou,
    Rocha, William,
    Passacrassana or Comice
175 g/6 oz sugar

125 g/4 oz butter
250 g/8 oz Puff Pastry
    (page 18)
300 ml/½ pt crème fraîche,
    to serve

Quarter, peel and core the pears. Toss the pears in a bowl with a few tablespoons of the sugar as you work. Melt the butter and sugar in a 24 cm/9½ in heavy cast-iron pan that is ovenproof (or you can caramelize the pears in a frying pan and then transfer them to a cake or flan tin). Arrange the pears in a layer over the butter. Cook over a high heat, uncovered, for about 20 minutes, until the sugar starts to caramelize and turn a deep golden brown. Leave to cool.

Heat the oven to 220°C/425°F/Gas Mark 7.

Roll out a thin circle of pastry slightly larger than the pan you are using. Place the pastry on top of the pears, tucking the dough around the edges. Bake for 10 minutes or until the pastry is golden brown. Lower the heat to 180°C/350°F/Gas Mark 4 and bake for a further 10–15 minutes. Cool the tart slightly and place a large heatproof dish on top of the tart. Using oven gloves, invert the pan smartly so that the tart falls on to the serving dish. If any pears stick to the bottom of the pan remove them with a spatula and replace on the tart.** Serve warm with the crème fraîche.

Note: The tart can successfully be reheated in a moderate oven for about 15 minutes.

VARIATION
Replace the pears with Cox apples and you have the original version.

** *Can be prepared in advance up to this point.*

Rhubarb Tart

This tart is only successful if made with young small pink or red rhubarb. The thick green stalks are too acidic and lack flavour.

SERVES 6–8

Sweet Shortcrust Pastry
　(page 20)
750 g/1½ lb rhubarb, cut
　into 2.5 cm/1 in pieces
175 g/6 oz soft brown sugar

2 eggs
300 ml/½ pt double cream
75 g/3 oz caster sugar

Roll out and line a 25 cm/10 in flan tin with the pastry. Chill until firm then prick the bottom with a fork.

Place a baking sheet in the oven and heat to 180°C/350°F/Gas Mark 4.

Put the rhubarb into the pastry case in an even layer and sprinkle with the brown sugar. Bake for 20 minutes.

Lower the heat to 150°C/300°F/Gas Mark 2.

Mix together the eggs, cream and caster sugar and pour them over the rhubarb. Cook for a further 20 minutes. Remove from the oven and allow to cool slightly before serving warm.

Flourless Chocolate Cake

This very special flourless cake is light and moist with the unique advantage of having one mixture serve as both cake and frosting.

SERVES 10–12

300 g/10 oz plain or
    bittersweet chocolate
125 g/4 oz butter
7 free-range egg yolks
150 g/5 oz caster sugar
1 tablespoon creme de cacao
    or dark rum

salt
6 free-range egg whites
cocoa for dusting
250 ml/8 fl oz whipping
    cream, whipped, to serve

Butter and flour a 20 cm/8 in cake tin and line the bottom with baking parchment.

Heat the oven to 170°C/325°F/Gas Mark 3.

Melt the chocolate and butter together in the top of a double saucepan set over a pan of hot but not boiling water.

Meanwhile, whisk the egg yolks and two-thirds of the sugar until they are thick and light in colour. Fold the chocolate mixture into the egg yolks and add the alcohol and a pinch of salt.

Whisk the egg whites with another small pinch of salt until the soft peak stage. Add the remaining sugar and continue to whisk until stiff peaks have formed. First fold a few tablespoons of the whites into the chocolate mixture to lighten it before folding in the rest.

Spoon about three-quarters of the batter into the cake tin and smooth the top level with a spatula; refrigerate the rest. Bake for 45 minutes. Leave in the tin for 10 minutes before running a knife around the edge and carefully turning it out on to a cake rack. When the cake is cool, invert it on to a serving dish. The top may be slightly cracked but this is normal.

Cover the cake with the remaining chocolate mixture.** Sieve a fine layer of cocoa over the top before serving. Serve with whipped cream.

** *Can be prepared in advance up to this point.*

Chocolate Mousse Cake

More a mousse than a cake, this is one of those desserts that make chocolate lovers gasp with pleasure after the first melting mouthful. It takes no time to make but does need to be assembled with care. Continental cooking chocolate is now available in supermarkets. It has a cocoa solid content of around 75 per cent and it is bitter. It can improve the chocolate flavour in most recipes but the required amount of sugar may need adjusting.

SERVES 10–12

250 g/8 oz dark cooking chocolate	2 tablespoons cognac or brandy
75 g/3 oz continental dark cooking chocolate	unsweetened cocoa powder, sifted
600 ml/1 pt double cream	crème fraîche, to serve (optional)
2 tablespoons milk	

Lightly grease a 24–25 cm/9 ½–10 in cake tin and line the bottom with baking parchment.

Break both the chocolates into small pieces and place them in the top of a double saucepan set over hot water. Cover and leave until the chocolate has melted. Stir the chocolate and let stand until it has cooled to blood temperature.

Place the container of cream in a bowl of hot water until it is just cool but not cold. Whisk the cream with the milk and cognac until it reaches the ribbon stage – when the whisk is lifted you can make a ribbon trail that will keep its shape. Do not over-whip. Fold the chocolate into the cream using a large metal spoon. Turn into the tin and smooth the top with a palette knife. Cover the tin with cling film and refrigerate for at least 1 hour or overnight.**

Before serving, slip a knife around the edge of the tin. Set the bottom of the tin in hot water for 10 seconds. This will just begin to melt the cake so that it will turn out with ease. Invert on to a serving plate. Remove the parchment paper disc, and smooth the top with a palette knife before sifting a fine covering of cocoa powder over the top of the cake. Leave at room temperature for 1–2 hours before serving. Serve with a bowl of crème fraîche passed separately.

** *Can be prepared in advance up to this point.*

Polenta Crumble Cake

This is a cross between crumble and shortbread and is delicious served with fruit or a glass of vin Santo.

SERVES 10

190 g/6½ oz plain flour
125 g/4 oz polenta flour
125 g/4 oz ground almonds
135 g/4½ oz caster sugar
½ teaspoon salt
grated rind of 2 unwaxed
    or well-washed lemons

2 large egg yolks
150 g/5 oz butter, at room
    temperature
icing sugar

Heat the oven to 190°C/375°F/Gas Mark 5. Grease a 25-cm/10-in cake tin.

Place the flour, polenta, almonds, sugar, salt and lemon zest in a bowl. Add the egg yolks and work with your fingers until it is incorporated into the dry ingredients. Cut the butter into small pieces and work again with your fingers until the mixture is moistened throughout by the butter and forms a coarse crumble.

Take handfuls of the mixture and crumble it with your fingertips into the prepared tin. Distribute it in an even layer over the tin but do not pat it down. Sprinkle the top with sifted icing sugar.

Bake for 40 minutes, or until the cake is golden brown.**

** *Can be prepared in advance.*

Mascarpone and Ginger Cheesecake

The syrup from stem ginger is used in the base of this cheesecake and makes it somewhere between pastry and ginger biscuits – a very good contrast with the smoothness of the mascarpone and cream cheese.

SERVES 8–10

For the pastry:
125 g/4 oz butter
50 g/2 oz caster sugar
200 g/7 oz flour
1 teaspoon ground ginger
1 tablespoon syrup from
   stem ginger
1 pinch of salt

For the filling:
500 g/1 1b full fat cream cheese
250 g/8 oz mascarpone cheese
175 g/6 oz caster sugar
2 large free-range eggs, beaten
125 g/4 oz stem ginger, chopped
5 cm/2 in piece of ginger root,
   grated

First prepare the crust base. Make the pastry either in a food processor or by hand and add as much water as necessary to form the dough into a ball. Wrap in cling film and chill for 30 minutes. Roll out the pastry to fit the bottom and 1 cm/½ in up the sides of a 25 × 5 cm/10 × 2 in tart tin with a removable base. Freeze for 1 hour.

Heat the oven to 220°C/425°F/Gas Mark 7 and bake the pastry for 25 minutes, then leave to cool.

Heat the oven to 150°C/300°F/Gas Mark 2 and put a large pan of hot water on the bottom rack. (This will stop a crust from forming on the cheesecake.)

Mix the cream cheese and mascarpone until smooth, then add the sugar. Pour in the eggs and stir well with both the gingers. Spread the mixture evenly over the crust and bake for 20 minutes on the rack above the tray of water. When it has almost set, remove the cheesecake from the oven and run a knife round the edge. Leave it to cool for about 10–15 minutes. Refrigerate for at least 2 hours.** Remove tin just before serving

** *Can be prepared in advance up to this point.*

Lemon Mousse Cheesecake

This is a memorable light-textured cheesecake with a very lemony flavour that has so far never failed to please. It needs several hours in the refrigerator so bake it the day before you need it.

SERVES 12

750 g/1½ lb full fat cream cheese, at room temperature
300 g/10 oz caster sugar
40 g/1½ oz flour
4 eggs, separated, at room temperature
150 ml/¼ pt lemon juice

grated rind of 2 large unwaxed or well-scrubbed lemons
1 pinch of salt
125 g/4 oz digestive biscuits or amaretti biscuits, crushed

Grease a 25 × 5 cm/10 × 2 in round cake tin and line the bottom with baking parchment. Preheat the oven to 170°C/325°F/Gas Mark 3.

Place the cream cheese in a large bowl and using an electric beater, beat until smooth. Gradually add 250 g/8 oz of the sugar and beat until light. Beat in the flour and then add the egg yolks, lemon juice and rind. Beat for about 1 minute, until the mixture is smooth.

Whisk the egg whites with a pinch of salt until you reach the soft peak stage. Add the remaining sugar and beat until the whites form stiff peaks. Carefully fold the egg whites into the cheese.

Pour the mixture into the pan and place it inside a larger pan or baking dish. Place the pans in the oven and pour enough hot water into the outer pan to come 2.5 cm/1 in up the side.

Bake until golden – about 60-65 minutes. Cool on a rack and then cover. Refrigerate for at least 4 hours or overnight.**

Run a knife around the inside edge. Place a flat plate, bottom side up, over the pan and invert on to the plate. Smooth the top of the cheesecake with a palette knife, dipping it frequently in very hot water. Sprinkle the crumbs over the top of the cake in an even layer, pressing down slightly to make a crust. Cut into slices with a hot sharp knife to serve.

** Can be prepared in advance up to this point.

Passion Fruit Mousse

A beautifully light and fragrant mousse that can be prepared ahead. If you can find leaf gelatine, it is preferable to powdered because it is practically tasteless. When buying passion fruit choose the smooth rather than the puckered ones – they are far juicier.

SERVES 6

20 passion fruit	2 egg whites
7 g/ ¼ oz powdered or leaf gelatine (2 × 5 ml teaspoons powdered)	1 pinch of salt
	65 g/2 ½ oz caster sugar
	150 ml/ ¼ pt whipping cream
juice of 1 lemon	icing sugar
1 ripe nectarine or peach	

Cut the passion fruit in half, scoop out the insides and place them in a blender. Blend on low speed for 1 minute to separate the flesh from the black seeds. Turn into a sieve and rub as much of the juice through as possible, scraping the bottom of the sieve a few times. Measure 175 ml/6 fl oz of the juice to use for the mousse. Add a few tablespoons of the black seeds to the remaining juice and set it aside for the sauce.

If you are using leaf gelatine, soften it in cold water for a few minutes. When it is flexible, shake off any excess water and place it in a cup with 2 tablespoons of the measured passion fruit juice and 2 tablespoons of lemon juice. Set the cup in a pan with warm water to come half-way up the side of the cup and heat gently until the gelatine has melted. If you are using powdered gelatine, sprinkle it over the same amount of juice, place in the cup and dissolve in the same way. Pour the gelatine mixture into the remaining passion fruit juice.

Skin the nectarine or peach, chop the flesh and purée. Add 100 g/3 ½ oz of the flesh to the passion fruit mixture. Add any remaining pulp to the sauce.

Whisk the egg whites and salt until stiff, add the sugar and whisk until the mixture is glossy and stiff. Lightly whip the cream. Carefully fold the cream into the egg whites, then fold in the passion fruit.

Spoon into 6 × 150 ml/ ¼ pt dariole moulds or a 1.2 L/2 pt soufflé dish lined with cling film. Refrigerate for at least 5 hours.**

** *Can be prepared in advance.*

Turn the mousse out and smooth any uneven surfaces with a palette knife. Add a few tablespoons of lemon juice to the sauce. Whisk in just enough sifted icing sugar to arrive at a sweet-tart taste. Spoon a little sauce over the top of each mousse before serving.

Ginger Custard

A silky-smooth ginger-flavoured custard.

SERVES 8

75 g/3 oz fresh ginger, peeled and finely chopped
4 tablespoons demerara sugar
350 ml/12 fl oz single cream

350 ml/12 fl oz milk
3 whole eggs
2 egg yolks
50 g/2 oz crystallized ginger, finely chopped

Place the fresh ginger and sugar in a saucepan and crush them together with a wooden spoon. Add the cream and milk and bring to just below boiling point. Cover and leave for 30 minutes to infuse.

Beat the eggs and yolks together. Strain the cream mixture over the eggs and mix together. Put aside 2 teaspoons of the crystallized ginger and divide the rest between 8 × 250 ml/8 fl oz ramekins.

Preheat the oven to 150°C/300°F/Gas Mark 2.

Place the custards in an oven pan filled with enough hot water to come half-way up the sides of the ramekins. Bake for 30 minutes or until set. When cool,** sprinkle the remaining ginger over the top and serve.

** *Can be prepared in advance up to this point.*

Chocolate Mousse with Candied Orange Peel

This must be the simplest and the best of all chocolate mousses. The quality of the chocolate is important; try to find one with 64 per cent cocoa solids, such as Valrhona or Nestlé Noir. Prepare at least 4 hours but not more than 8 hours before serving.

SERVES 6–8

200 g/7 oz good-quality
   dark chocolate
6 free-range eggs, separated
2 tablespoons Cointreau or
   Grand Marnier
1 pinch of salt

For the orange peel:
peel of 2 oranges
100 g/3 ½ oz sugar, plus extra
   for coating
5 tablespoons water

Break the chocolate into pieces and melt them in a bowl over hot water. Remove from the heat and stir in the egg yolks followed by the Cointreau or Grand Marnier.

Put a pinch of salt into the bowl with the egg whites and whip until they form soft peaks. With a metal spoon gently fold the egg whites into the chocolate.

Pour the mixture into individual ramekins or a large glass bowl. Chill for at least 3–4 hours.

Cut the peel into thin strips. Cover with cold water, bring to the boil, then drain. Repeat the process a few times until the peel is soft. Make a sugar syrup with the sugar and water. Boil the peel in the syrup until it is absorbed. Cool, roll in the sugar and dry on racks.** Sprinkle some of the peel over the mousse before serving. Store any extra in an airtight jar.

VARIATION:
Omit the orange peel and sprinkle some crushed amaretti biscuits into the ramekins before you fill them.

** *Can be prepared in advance up to this point.*

Geranium Cream with Blackberries

SERVES 4

300 ml/½ pt double cream   2 scented geranium leaves
2 tablespoons sugar   500 g/1 lb blackberries

Place the cream with the sugar and geranium leaves in the top of a double saucepan set over hot water. Heat, without allowing the cream to come to the boil, for 15 minutes or until the cream is well scented.** Cool, then lightly whip the cream and serve with the blackberries.

Blood Orange Sorbet

Both the rich red colour and the flavour of this orange sorbet are exceptional. It is something to look forward to when these oranges are in season in January.

SERVES 8
175 g/6 oz sugar   juice of 1 lemon
100 ml/3½ fl oz water   icing sugar (optional)
900 ml/1½ pt fresh blood
    orange juice (about 20
    oranges)

Over moderate heat, without stirring, dissolve the sugar in the water while bringing it to the boil. Boil for 2 minutes, then remove from the heat and leave to cool.

Mix the sugar syrup with the orange juice. Add a squeeze of lemon juice and test. You want a sharp yet sweet taste. Adjust the flavour by adding more lemon juice or whisking in a bit of sifted icing sugar.

Freeze in an ice-cream maker, if you have one. Otherwise pour the mixture into a metal container and set it in the freezer for about 3 hours. Chop the sorbet into chunks, place in a chilled processor bowl and process until smooth. Return to the container and freeze for at least another 3 hours.**

** *Can be prepared in advance.*

Cold Lemon Soufflé with Candied Lemon Slices

A shallow glass dish on a stem is ideal for this pudding as the lemon slices are then visible. If possible candy the lemons 24 hours before you want to use them.

SERVES 6–8

For the candied lemons:
250 g/8 oz caster sugar
125 ml/4 fl oz water
3 unwaxed lemons, cut into
   very fine slices

For the soufflé:
2 large lemons, grated rind
  and juice

15 g/scant ½ oz powdered or
   leaf gelatine (1 package
   of powdered)
150 g/5 oz caster sugar
4 large free-range eggs,
   separated
1 pinch of salt

Start by preparing the candied lemons. Bring the sugar and water to the boil in a medium-sized pan and boil until the syrup thickens slightly. Add the lemon slices, stir them gently to cover with the syrup and simmer for 5 minutes. Turn off the heat and leave them in the pan for 10 minutes. With a slotted spoon, remove the slices and drain them on a wire rack. Save and refrigerate the syrup for re-use with added sugar.

Pour the lemon juice into a small pan and sprinkle on the powdered gelatine. Leave it aside until needed. If you are using gelatine leaves, place them in cold water until soft, shake off the excess water and add to the lemon juice.

Place the sugar, egg yolks and lemon rind in a large bowl and whisk until the mixture is pale. Gently warm the lemon juice to heat the gelatine leaves or to melt the powdered gelatine, but do not allow it to boil. Whisk the hot lemon juice into the egg yolk mixture.

Sprinkle the salt on to the egg whites and whisk until they are firm, then fold them into the lemon mixture.

Line a glass dish with the candied lemon slices and pour the mixture into it. Refrigerate for 2–3 ** hours and when set arrange any remaining candied lemon slices on the top.

** *Can be prepared in advance up to this point.*

Pears in Red Wine with Prunes and Dried Cherries

This is a dish that should be prepared well in advance as considerable time has to be allowed for the cooling. The red pears in the dark glossy syrup look wonderful served in a glass bowl.

SERVES 4

12 large prunes, stoned	1 cinnamon stick
6 firm ripe pears	6 cloves
750 ml/1 ¼ pt full-bodied red wine	2 bay leaves
175 g/6 oz sugar	50 g/2 oz dried cherries
2 teaspoons black peppercorns	zest of 1 scrubbed lemon
½ freshly grated nutmeg	5-cm/2-in piece of fresh ginger, finely chopped

Soak the prunes in just enough cold water to cover them for at least 6 hours.

Peel the pears, leaving them whole, and place them stem upwards in a deep pan into which they should fit snugly. Pour in the wine, sugar, spices and bay leaves. Bring gently to the boil and cover. Simmer for 15 minutes, then add the drained prunes and the cherries. Continue cooking for a further 10 minutes. Remove from the heat and leave to cool in the cooking liquid.

Remove the pears, prunes and cherries from the pan and arrange them on a dish with the pear stems upwards. Reduce the wine until it is syrupy and add the lemon zest and ginger. Pick out and discard the peppercorns, cinnamon stick, bay leaves and cloves.** When the liquid has cooled, pour it over the pears and prunes. Serve cold.

** *Can be prepared in advance up to this point.*

Quince Paste with Ricotta

Quince paste, 'Dulce de Membrillo', is a treat to bring back from Spain. A slice or two served with ricotta or cream cheese makes a delicious dessert. If you can find the quinces it is easy to make your own paste, and it will keep well for months.

SERVES 8

1 kg/2 lb quinces	granulated sugar
125 ml/4 fl oz water	350 g/12 oz ricotta cheese

To make the quince paste, wash the quinces and cut them into chunks, discarding any black flower tips. Place in a heavy saucepan with the water. Cover and simmer gently until soft, about 20 minutes. Press through a food *mouli* or sieve.

Measure the purée, and add 275 g/9 oz of sugar to every 500 g/1 lb of purée. Rinse out the pan, add the sugar and purée, and cook over a very gentle heat, stirring occasionally, until the purée comes away from the sides and bottom of the pan. As the mixture gets thicker, keep an eye on it and stir more frequently so that it does not catch and burn.

Line a 20 × 30 cm/8 × 12 in tin with baking parchment. Pour the mixture into the tin and spread it level with a palette knife. Leave in a warm place for 24 hours. If it is not quite firm enough, turn it out on to another piece of baking parchment. Remove the top piece and leave for another 24 hours so that the other side can dry out.**

Place a few squares of quince paste with a slice or two of very fresh ricotta on individual dessert plates.

** *Can be prepared in advance up to this point.*

Ricotta and Coffee Cream

This tradition Italian dessert couldn't be simpler to make and is delicious served with Cantuccii (page 210).

SERVES 4

250 g/8 oz ricotta cheese
50 g/2 oz mascarpone
   cheese
75 g/3 oz caster sugar
3 tablespoons rum
   (optional)

3 teaspoons ground
   espresso coffee
grated bitter chocolate, to
   decorate

Place the ricotta, mascarpone and sugar in the bowl of a food processor and blend until smooth. Add the rum and coffee and whiz briefly. Spoon into individual ramekins and chill for at least 2 hours.**

Sprinkle with the chocolate before serving.

Ricotta Pudding

If you are in Italy and can find ewe's milk ricotta this dessert will be even more delicious. It still tastes very good made with the freshest cow's milk ricotta you can buy. If you don't have vanilla extract or essence, keep a few vanilla pods in a covered jar of caster sugar to make vanilla sugar. Use it to sprinkle over this pudding and use it in other recipes calling for vanilla.

SERVES 6

350 g/12 oz fresh ricotta
   cheese
1 large orange
50 g/2 oz ground almonds
50 g/2 oz sifted icing sugar
25 g/1 oz sultanas

2 egg yolks (optional)
1 teaspoon vanilla extract
   (not flavouring)
granulated sugar, for
   decorating

Push the ricotta through a sieve or blend in a food processor. Turn into a bowl. Remove the zest from a well-washed orange with a potato peeler and chop finely. Mix the zest, almonds, icing sugar, sultanas, egg yolks and vanilla into the ricotta.** Before serving sprinkle the top with granulated sugar.

** *Can be prepared in advance up to this point.*

Cantuccii

If you are serving fruit at the end of a meal it is often nice to set it off by serving a dessert wine and a basket of dry Italian cantuccii biscuits. In Italy they are dunked into the vin Santo but they are delicious softened in any sweet wine. They are simple to make and keep indefinitely.

MAKES ABOUT 4 DOZEN

250 g/8 oz strong flour
175 g/6 oz plain flour, plus
    extra if needed
1 teaspoon baking powder
½ teaspoon salt
275 g/9 oz caster sugar
2 teaspoons aniseed
finely chopped zest of 1
    large orange

3 eggs
3 egg yolks
1 teaspoon real vanilla
    extract
200 g/7 oz whole
    unbleached almonds

Heat the oven to 160°C/325°F/Gas Mark 3.

Sift the strong flour, plain flour, baking powder and salt into a large bowl. Stir in the sugar, aniseed and orange zest. Make a well in the centre and pour in the eggs, egg yolks and vanilla. Mix only enough to form a sticky dough and then add the almonds. Turn out on to a floured surface and roll into three logs, each about 25 × 5 cm/ 10 × 2 in, using some of the remaining flour if necessary.

Line a baking sheet with baking parchment and set the logs on it with a good space in between them. Bake for 20 minutes. When cool, cut the logs at a slight angle into 2 cm/¾ in thick slices.

Lower the oven temperature to 150°C/300°F/Gas Mark 2.

Place the biscuits on two baking sheets and bake for a further 20–25 minutes, until golden brown. Cool on racks. Store in an airtight container.**

** *Can be prepared in advance.*

INDEX